THE NEW YORK P

An Anthology

MARK FORD was born in 1962. His publications include two collections of poetry, *Landlocked* (Chatto & Windus, 1992, 1998), and *Soft Sift* (Faber & Faber, 2001 / Harcourt Brace, 2003); a critical biography of the French poet, playwright and novelist Raymond Roussel (*Raymond Roussel and the Republic of Dreams*, Faber & Faber, 2000 / Cornell University Press, 2001); a 20,000 word interview with John Ashbery (Between the Lines, 2003) and, for Carcanet, *The New York Poets*, an anthology of poems by Frank O'Hara, John Ashbery, Kenneth Koch and James Schuyler (2003), and *'Why I Am Not a Painter' and other poems*, a selection of the poetry of Frank O'Hara (2003). Mark Ford is a regular contributor to the *Times Literary Supplement* and the *London Review of Books*. He teaches in the English department at University College, London.

TREVOR WINKFIELD was born in Leeds in 1944. He exhibits his paintings at the Tibor de Nagy Gallery, New York, with whom he has also published a collaboration with Kenward Elmslie, *Snippets* (Tibor de Nagy Editions, 2002). *Trevor Winkfield's Drawings* (Bamberger Books, 2004) lists and illustrates his other collaborations with New York School poets. He is the editor and translator of Raymond Roussel's *How I Wrote Certain of my Books and Other Writings* (Exact Change, 1955).

Also from Carcanet

The New York Poets: An Anthology, edited by Mark Ford

John Ashbery
And the Stars Were Shining
April Galleons
Can You Hear Bird
Chinese Whispers
Flow Chart
Girls on the Run
Hotel Lautréamont
The Mooring of Starting Out
Reported Sightings
Selected Poems
Self-Portrait in a Convex Mirror
Wakefulness
A Wave
Your Name Here
with James Schuyler
A Nest of Ninnies

Barbara Guest
Selected Poems

Kenneth Koch
One Train
Selected Poems

Harry Mathews
A Mid Season Sky

Frank O'Hara
Selected Poems
'Why I Am Not a Painter' and other poems, edited by Mark Ford

James Schuyler
Selected Poems

THE NEW YORK POETS II

An Anthology

Edited with an introduction by
MARK FORD and TREVOR WINKFIELD

First published in Great Britain in 2006 by
Carcanet Press Limited
Alliance House
Cross Street
Manchester M2 7AQ

Acknowledgements of permission to reprint in-copyright material can be found on pp. 216–16 and constitute an extension of the copyright page.

A CIP catalogue record for this book is available from the British Library
ISBN 1 85754 821 3
978 1 85754 821 1

The publisher acknowledges financial assistance from Arts Council England

Typeset by XL Publishing Services, Tiverton
Printed and bound in England by SRP Ltd, Exeter

CONTENTS

Edwin Denby

Barbara Guest

Kenward Elmslie

Harry Mathews

Ted Berrigan

Joseph Ceravolo

Bill Berkson

Clark Coolidge

Charles North

Ron Padgett

Bernadette Mayer

INTRODUCTION

'We lived through a golden age . . . and didn't know it!' exclaimed Kenward Elmslie after perusing the revelatory exhibition *A Secret Location on the Lower East Side*. Held at New York's Public Library in 1998, the show was devoted to 'Adventures in Writing, 1960–1980', and clarified beyond any accusation of nostalgia the mounting suspicion that American poetry (particularly that emanating from New York) had at that time (and more or less in tandem with the art world) enjoyed a period of genuine excitement, experimentation and achievement.

The 1960s in particular proved a watershed, full of arrivals and departures. Arriving were the reputations of Frank O'Hara, John Ashbery, James Schuyler and Kenneth Koch; departing were the younger poets who took off from them. For it wasn't until the 1960s that the underground reputations of what came to be known as the New York School of Poets began to emerge as influences; previously ignored or lightly dismissed as eccentric, they seemed destined to expire without issue, like those other valiant mavericks of American poetry, Lorine Niedecker and John Wheelwright. Though the New York School soon came to be seen as a distinct body, like any other entity it had correlations with other groups, fed off them, outgrew them, and eventually gave rise to rival groups who repudiated their supposed aims. And the irony is, it was never a school: no desks or manifestos are anywhere to be found (aside from O'Hara's spoof one, 'Personism'), no rules and regulations were ever drafted, and applications were never sought – except from the impecunious Ted Berrigan, who used to tell innocents they could join if they gave him five dollars. They never set out to change the world like the Futurists or Surrealists, or circulated a party line on political or aesthetic issues. What all adherents did share, however, was a rare mixture of high seriousness leavened with a sense of humour, and a faith in the acrobatic capabilities of language.

There could have been no more apt location for this updated version of Babel than the polyglot, multicultural New York of the 1960s, where English was spoken in several languages, 'where sometimes,' as Ron Padgett once put it, 'you gotta schlep down to the bodega for some chow mein.' The circumambient mongrelisation of language made writers exactingly conscious of their own dialects and idioms, and the underside of all language systems, as Harry Mathews amusingly illustrates in his phonetic parody of the alphabet:

Crow to Scarecrow

Hay, be seedy! Effigy! Hate-shy, jaky yellow man,
O peek, you are rusty, you've edible, you ex-wise head!

This was a period when New York was becoming a truly international city, as opposed to a merely cosmopolitan one. It had of course historically long been an immigrant destination, but in the 1960s it became a target for the creative young as never before. To an extent New York's rise to pre-eminence was the result of the post-war decline of Paris, which, after the global triumph of Abstract Expressionism, could no longer claim to be the artistic centre of the Western world. Surrounding and abutting the painters, in ever widening circles, spread the music of John Cage, Morton Feldman and Christian Wolff; happenings by Alan Kaprow, Red Grooms, and Claes Oldenburg; and underground movies by Rudy Burckhardt and Jack Smith. Perhaps what most fuelled the fervent desire of young would-be artists was the intense cross-pollination between the arts. Painters made covers for little reviews, built stage-sets for plays, and then acted in them. Musicians provided soundtracks for underground movies, which poets starred in. Dancers went to poetry readings, and poets became art critics, reviewing shows all and sundry trooped to see. Poets and painters collaborated on sets of lithographs and comic strips, and frequently alluded to, and even borrowed wholesale each other's work. Jasper Johns's *Screen Piece* of 1968 has a Ted Berrigan sonnet affixed to it, while Larry Rivers's 1977 portrait of John Ashbery includes just about the entire text of 'Pyrography'. References to painters such as Fairfield Porter, Jane Freilicher and Joe Brainard pop up in poem after poem by Schuyler, Berrigan, Koch, Padgett and O'Hara. Everyone, it seemed, knew everyone, and nobody talked about pursuing an artistic career, though with hindsight it turns out that's exactly what – consciously or not – all were doing.

Life in the 1960s was, if not 'incredibly cheap' as legend now has it, at least very affordable. It was perhaps the last occasion when designations such as 'avant-garde' and 'bohemian' had relevance, when artists could move to the city en masse – a city become as dark, mysterious and as dangerous as the Paris of Gérard de Nerval and Baudelaire – before New York reverted to its accustomed role as a business centre. Rents especially were low ('You have to be insane to want to live here' – i.e. an artist – as the saying went), and artists needed to work only two or three days a week in order to generate a subsistence income. Some found ways to avoid even that commitment to wage slavery.

Kenneth Koch once hailed Ted Berrigan as 'sort of the daddy of the downtown poets, taking care of everybody and showing them what it was like to be a poet'. Berrigan's life perfectly exemplifies why poets flocked to New York. A couple of extracts from his journal of 1963 capture the love-hate, heaven-hell relationship most New York poets have towards their chosen abode, and why they are ultimately willing to tolerate so much discomfort in order to remain there:

> I still feel at low level. No drive. Financial problems the main cause and the prospect of going to work. The rent is 3 days overdue today. $13.50. I have $1.00 and [am] faced with selling my Collected Poems of Wallace Stevens. God damn it! (January 3rd)

> Went to a cocktail party at Larry Rivers's studio at the Chelsea Hotel given by Larry for Frank O'Hara's return from Europe – talked to Edwin [Denby] and later went to eat with Barbara Guest and Joe Brainard and Barney Newman and his wife . . . (December 2nd)

Berrigan lived the typical New York bohemian life – poor, yet with exhilarating access to a vigorous intellectual life and exciting social events (as long as he was prepared to walk home afterwards for want of a subway token).

Not all the poets assembled in this anthology were devoid of funds. Several came from wealthy backgrounds, and proved extremely generous to their more impoverished colleagues. But both sides of the economic fence were beneficiaries of the break up of the old class barriers that had dogged America up until the 1960s, allowing a mingling that would have perturbed an earlier generation. For artists at any rate, the city was for a while a genuine melting pot. Though not all poets associated with the New York School lived there on a permanent basis, most did so, and even long-term expatriates such as John Ashbery and Harry Mathews managed to keep in touch with the scene through regular letters and irregular visits. Those who formed the nucleus of the group lived within walking distance of each other, in Greenwich Village, or the East Village, or Chelsea, while the area around St Mark's Church in the Bowery functioned much like Montmartre or Bloomsbury had in their heydays, as a kind of Equator.

Although the reading series hosted in the early 60s at the cafés Les Deux

Mégots (on East Seventh St,) and Le Metro (on Second Avenue between Ninth and Tenth) were important in bringing together all sorts of poets who shared a basic dislike of Establishment or academic poetry (summed up for many by the work of the much despised Robert Lowell), it was the St Mark's Poetry Project that played the most crucial role in defining the group's sense of identity. The Project was started in 1966 with the aid of a grant from the Health, Education, and Welfare Office of Juvenile Delinquency and Development. The church received around $200,000 to initiate a series of readings and workshops ostensibly intended to lure 'alienated youth' back into 'mainstream culture'; it quickly developed, however, into a forum for a wide range of dissident poetic voices. Most of the poets included in this volume took part in the Project's reading series (which forty years on is still going strong), appeared in its magazine *The World*, and some, such as Ted Berrigan, Ron Padgett, and Bernadette Mayer ran highly influential workshops there.

The St Mark's Poetry Project was also, though, hospitable to Beat poets such as Allen Ginsberg, Peter Orlovsky, and Ed Sanders (editor of *Fuck You / a magazine of the arts* and lead singer of the rock group The Fugs), and would eventually prove important to the evolution of writers such as Charles Bernstein and Bruce Andrews associated with the magazine *L=A=N=G=U=A=G=E* and its offshoots. All kinds of tribes and factions proliferated within the alternative poetry scene of 1960s New York; and while everyone, it almost goes without saying, opposed the war in Vietnam, some such as Ginsberg and Sanders believed poetry could be made into a direct and effective form of political activism, whereas, at the other extreme, Kenneth Koch for instance found himself quite incapable of producing a protest poem, as he frankly acknowledged in 'The Pleasures of Peace' (1969): 'to my contemporaries I'll leave the horrors of the war / they can do them better than I.'

Donald Allen's pathbreaking anthology of 1960, *The New American Poetry*, divided its contributors into five sections: Black Mountain, San Francisco Renaissance, Beat, the New York Poets, and a catch-all section for younger poets. In practice the boundaries between these groupings were at least partially permeable, and certainly the generation of poets schooled on Allen, who began writing and publishing in the 1960s, had no qualms about borrowing from Charles Olson or Gregory Corso or Robert Duncan whatever concept or device or turn of phrase they coveted, collaging or fusing their influences as poets always do. Nevertheless, Allen's divisions proved useful at the time, and remain so. His section of New York poets featured the work of six poets (Ashbery, O'Hara, Koch, Schuyler, Guest and Edward Field); the following year John Bernard Myers published an article in the Californian magazine *Nomad* labelling this group 'The New York School of Poets', and for better or worse, and despite the exasperated protests of many of the poets thus pigeon-holed, the term has remained current ever since.

This volume, and its predecessor *The New York Poets: An Anthology* (2004), do not, it must be stressed, attempt to represent the range of poets at work in New York in the period 1950–80 (the decades from which most of the poems in both books are drawn). The idea, rather, was to make available to British readers selections from writers whose work falls roughly under the aegis of New York School ideals and practices. Although these are not easy to define, few readers will have trouble discerning the relationship between, say, Charles North and John Ashbery, or Bill Berkson and Frank O'Hara; most of the poets knew each other, many collaborated together, and to a lesser or greater extent all participated in an evolving poetic community that the St Mark's Poetry Project semi-institutionalised.

The 1970 anthology, *The New York Poets*, edited by Ron Padgett and David Shapiro, included the work of twenty-seven poets, and Terry Diggory's forthcoming *Encyclopedia of New York Poets* provides entries on a staggering sixty-six poets. The eleven featured here, then, should be considered as offering only a slice of the action, a glimpse into the ways in which a certain strand within the alternative poetry scene in New York developed a shared set of artistic assumptions.

It has become customary to divide the New York School into its first and second generations: the first generation – Barbara Guest, Frank O'Hara, John Ashbery, Kenneth Koch, James Schuyler, Kenward Elmslie, Edwin Denby, Harry Mathews – all began writing in the aftermath of World War II, and in the twilight of Modernism: they sought ways of coming to terms with, and then moving beyond the achievements of Williams, Stevens, Eliot, Pound, Joyce, Auden, Stein, H.D., and Marianne Moore. The second generation, represented here by Ted Berrigan, Joseph Ceravolo, Bill Berkson, Clark Coolidge, Charles North, Ron Padgett, and Bernadette Mayer had, as well as the Modernists, the work of the first generation to absorb, challenge, and make use of. It might be argued that they in turn inspired a third generation, exemplified by the work of, say, Peter Gizzi or Chris Edgar, but in fact by the mid-1980s the kinds of experiment pioneered by both first and second generations had become so widely disseminated and imitated by poets all over America – and, it should be said, in Britain, Europe, and Australia also – that attempts to trace the genealogy further become hopelessly blurred and imprecise.

Until relatively recently academic criticism has focused mainly on the work of Ashbery and O'Hara, but with the publication of David Lehman's *The Last Avant-Garde: The Making of the New York School of Poets* (1998) and Daniel Kane's *All Poets Welcome: The Lower East Side Poetry Scene in the 1960s* (2003), which comes with a CD culled from recordings of readings at venues such as Le Metro and St Mark's, this has begun to change. Both books convey a sense of the extent to which New York writers of both generations figured poetry as a collaborative enterprise, and offer valuable discussions of the importance of magazines such as *Locus Solus* (edited by Ashbery, Schuyler, Mathews and Koch), *C: A Journal of Poetry* (edited by Berrigan), *The World* (edited by Anne Waldman), and *Angel Hair* (edited by Waldman and Lewis Warsh). The 1960s were the age of the mimeograph, which allowed magazines like *C* and *Angel Hair* to be assembled informally, quickly, and cheaply. Distributed mainly for free among friends, these magazines preserve an immediate, up-to-the-minute record of the community's activities and productions, and perfectly reflected their conception of poetry as something potentially happening anywhere all the time.

'I myself like the climate of New York,' observed Edwin Denby in the first poem of his first collection, *In Public, In Private* (1948), with which this book opens. Responding to and charting New York's climate – intellectual, aesthetic, moral, social, and political as well as meteorological – is one of the major preoccupations of the poets included in this volume. For some this involves referring to particular squares or streets, but in general these poems bear out the old cliché that New York is a state of mind. The states of mind dramatised here are not easy to categorise: they range from the delicate texturings of consciousness orchestrated by Barbara Guest to the explosive pop iconography of Kenward Elmslie; from the plangent lyricism of Joseph Ceravolo to the cool experiments in epistemology of Clark Coolidge; from the chiselled formal rigour of Edwin Denby to the casual, confiding expansiveness of Ted Berrigan – these last two, it's worth pointing out, both committed to reinvigorating that ur-form of lyric forms, the sonnet. And yet, for all their many differences, it seems to us the work of these poets gains considerably when restored to its original contexts, and seen as engaged with the dilemmas and ideals, the tensions and energies, the ferment of experiment and interaction that characterised what Peter Gizzi has called 'a foundational moment in American poetry'.

Mark Ford
Trevor Winkfield
2006

EDWIN DENBY

Edwin Denby was born in 1903 in Tientsin in China, where his father was the American Consul. He had a peripatetic upbringing; his father's diplomatic postings included spells in Hannover, Shanghai, and six years in Vienna, where Denby learned German and saw his first ballet. The family returned to America shortly after the outbreak of World War I. He attended schools in Detroit and Connecticut, and arrived at Harvard when he was only sixteen, having scored the highest marks in that year's college entrance exams in the country. However, he found university life not to his taste. He abandoned Harvard in the middle of his first year, and spent his twenties mainly back in Vienna; there he studied dance, founded a touring dance company, and composed numerous libretti, plays, and stories in German. In the course of this European sojourn he met Bertolt Brecht, Kurt Weill, Aaron Copland, and Virgil Thomson. He also saw his first performance of a Balanchine dance. Soon after his return to America in 1934 he began reviewing dance for *Modern Music*. His analyses, described by Lincoln Kirstein as 'glowing with an absolute love of the art', constitute the fullest and most illuminating record we have of the evolution of dance in New York in the 1940s and 50s. His various collections of reviews have become, to quote Kirstein again, 'basic theatrical history'.

Denby was notoriously modest about his own poetry. His first two collections, *In Public, In Private* (1948) and *Mediterranean Cities* (1956) were issued almost secretly by tiny presses, although the latter eventually received an excited review from Frank O'Hara in *Poetry*, which praised his work as 'modern and intrinsic, sensitive and strong'. In 1963 Ted Berrigan published a special Edwin Denby edition of *C*, and his *Collected Poems* of 1986 features an introduction by Ron Padgett and jacket copy by John Ashbery and James Schuyler. Without the determined championing of his work by these poets it seems unlikely it would have reached an audience beyond his own circle of friends and admirers. As Padgett notes in his introduction, Denby's poems can at first seem 'elusive, eccentric, or awkward', but after prolonged immersion 'one gradually acquires a sense of their wholeness, and particular craft behind that wholeness'. His sonnets are dense and labyrinthine, full of startling juxtapositions and disjunctions, while longer poems such as 'Snoring in New York – An Elegy' fuse an almost metaphysical complexity of thought with a pressing awareness of time and the quotidian. Denby's poetry is both original and compelling, and it had a significant influence on both generations of New York School poets. 'He sees and hears more clearly than anyone else I have ever known,' declared Frank O'Hara. Denby died in 1983.

The Climate

I myself like the climate of New York
I see it in the air up between the street
You use a worn-down cafeteria fork
But the climate you don't use stays fresh and neat.
Even we people who walk about in it
We have to submit to wear too, get muddy,
Air keeps changing but the nose ceases to fit
And sleekness is used up, and the end's shoddy.
Monday, you're down; Tuesday, dying seems a fuss
An adult looks new in the weather's motion
The sky is in the streets with the trucks and us,
Stands awhile, then lifts across land and ocean.
We can take it for granted that here we're home
In our record climate I look pleased or glum.

The Subway

The subway flatters like the dope habit,
For a nickel extending peculiar space:
You dive from the street, holing like a rabbit,
Roar up a sewer with a millionaire's face.

Squatting in the full glare of the locked express
Imprisoned, rocked, like a man by a friend's death,
O how the immense investment soothes distress,
Credit laps you like a huge religious myth.

It's a sound effect. The trouble is seeing
(So anaesthetized) a square of bare throat
Or the fold at the crotch of a clothed human being:
You'll want to nuzzle it, crop at it like a goat.

That's not in the buy. The company between stops
Offers you security, and free rides to cops.

City Without Smoke

Over Manhattan island when gales subside
Inhuman colors of ocean afternoons
Luminously livid, tear the sky so wide
The exposed city looks like deserted dunes.
Peering out to the street New Yorkers in saloons
Identify the smokeless moment outside
Like a subway stop where one no longer stirs. Soon
This oceanic gracefulness will have died.
For to city people the smudgy film of smoke
Is reassuring like an office, it's sociable
Like money, it gives the sky a furnished look
That makes disaster domestic, negotiable.
Nothing to help society in the sky's grace
Except that each looks at it with his mortal face.

Summer

I stroll on Madison in expensive clothes, sour.
Ostrich-legg'd or sweet-chested, the loping clerks
Slide me a glance nude as oh in a tiled shower
And lope on dead-pan, large male and female jerks.

Later from the open meadow in the Park
I watch a bulging pea-soup storm lie midtown;
Here the high air is clear, there buildings are murked,
Manhattan absorbs the cloud like a sage-brush plain.

In the grass sleepers sprawl without attraction:
Some large men who turned sideways, old ones on papers,
A soldier, face handkerchiefed, an erection
In his pants—only men, the women don't nap here.

Can these wide spaces suit a particular man?
They can suit whomever man's intestines can.

People on Sunday

In the street young men play ball, else in fresh shirts
Expect a girl, bums sit quietly soused in house-doors,
Girls in dresses walk looking ahead, a car starts
As the light clicks, and Greeks laugh in cafes upstairs.

Sundays the long asphalt looks dead like a beach
The heat lies on New York the size of the city
The season keeps moving through and out of reach
And people left in the kitchen are a little flighty.

Look at all the noises we make for one another
Like: shake cake bake take, or: ton gun run fun,
Like: the weather, the system, the picture of his brother,
And: shake hands and leave and look at the sun go down.

One Sunday a day-old baby looked right at my eyes
And turned its head away without the least surprise.

Aaron

Aaron had a passion for the lost chord. He looked for it under the newspapers at the Battery, saying to himself, "So many things have been lost." He was very logical and preferred to look when nobody was watching, as anyone would have, let us add. He was no crank, though he was funny somehow in his bedroom. He was so funny that everybody liked him, and hearing this those who had been revolted by him changed their minds. They were right to be pleasant, and if it hadn't been for something making them that way, they wouldn't have been involved in the first place. Being involved of course was what hurt. "It's a tight squeeze," Aaron was saying in his bedroom, and let us suppose he was quite right. He closed his eyes and shivered, enjoying what he did. And he went on doing it, until it was time for something else, saying "I like it." And he did. He liked a good tune too, if it lasted. He once remarked to somebody, "Tunes are like birds." He wanted to say it again, but he couldn't remember, so the conversation became general, and he didn't mind. What was Aaron's relationship to actuality? I think it was a very good relationship.

A Domestic Cat

The cat I live with is an animal
Conceived as I, though next to me she's small.
More like each other, so our births assert,
Than either one is like a house, or shirt.
I nervous at my table,
She by the stove and stable,
Show what a gap lies between cats and men;
But shift the point of view to see again
Surrounding both of us disgusting death,
Death frames us then in this still room, each pumping breath.

Her white fur where she cleaned it smells like talc;
Her claws can tap the floor in a rapid walk;
Her shape in walking bulges up and down;
Jealous, she sits remote, but does not frown.
To sleep, she puts an eye
Upside down next a thigh
And lost the small snout grows a deeper pink;
To eat, above the neck her elbows shrink,
The outstretched neck, the head tilt when she chews,
They thrust, they gulp; and sated she rises to refuse.

Compelled, as men by God are, twice each year
Her look turned stony, she will disappear;
Exhausted, three days later, dirty and plain
She will creep home, and be herself again.
She cleans her young contented,
At one month they're presented,
Clear-eyed she hauls them out and on my bed;
Here, while they wolf her tits, she purrs, outspread.
She waves her tail, they look, they leap, they riot,
She talks. And later, when they've gone, she cowers quiet.

Graceful as the whole sky, which time goes through,
Through going time she wanders, graceful too.
Sits in the sun, sleeps rounded on a chair,
Answers my voice with a green limpid stare.
Modest in drooping furs
She folds her paws and purrs
Charmed by the curious song of friendly talk;
But hearing up the stair a stamping walk,
Under the bed she streaks, weakly disgraced,
As humble as an alleycat that's being chased.

We live through time. I'll finish with a dream:
Wishing to play and bored, so she did seem;
But said, she knew two kittens just outside
That she could play with any time she tried;
We went to see this thing,
But one hung by a string,
A kitten strung up high, and that looked dead;
But when I took it down, it was well instead.
All three then played and had a pleasant time.
So at war dreamt a soldier; for him I made this rhyme.

Northern Boulevard

The bench, the sewermouth, the hydrant placed
On the street are attractive and foolproof,
Their finish is in republican taste
The expense, on democratic behoof.

People wear the city, the section they use
Like the clothes on their back and their hygiene
And they recognize property as they do news
By when to stay out and where to go in.

Near where a man keeps his Sunday plyers
Or young men play regularly, they place
Next to acts of financial empires
An object as magic as a private face.

No use to distinguish between hope and despair
Anyone's life is greater than his care.

Trastevere
A Dedication

Dear head to one side, in summer dusk, Olga
On her terrace waters potted azaleas
Thoughts of friends, their fine successes, their failures
Greek reliefs, Russian poets, all water with her;
The plants rejoice; across the street, the high wall
Reaches the decayed park of a long dead Pope
Urchins stole the sphinx near the fence up the hill
Where woods grow thick, sold it to a Yank I hope;
Now young priests smoke at the basin, by blurred sea-gods
Above them rises a hairy thicket of palms
That male in their joint green dusk yield Rome the odds
Returning with the night into primeval realms
As laughing Olga, feeding through the window cat-shadows
Then reading, then sinking into slumber, too does

Sant' Angelo d'Ischia

Wasps between my bare toes crawl and tickle; black
Sparkles sand on a white beach; ravines gape wide
Pastel-hued twist into a bare mountain's back
To boiling springs; emblems of earth's age are displayed;
At a distant end of beach white arcs piled
Windows, and in the sea a dead pyramid washed
As if in the whole world few people had survived
And man's sweetness had survived a grandeur extinguished;
Wonders of senility; I watch astonished
The old hermit poke with a stick the blond lame boy
Speaking obscenities, smiling weird and ravished
Who came from New York to die twenty years ago;
So at a wild farmer's cave we pour wine together
On a beach, four males in a brilliant weather

Delos

Dark pure blue, deep in the light, the sea shakes white-flecked
Foam-white houses sink, hills as dry as dried fruit
In a gale, in a radiance massive like sex
The boat bounces us and Greeks in business suits;
A thick-built landing stage; an isle low and small
And one old hill on it, cake-shapen; screening
The solitude other islands bulge and sprawl
She lies dazzled, floating, as remote as meaning;
Left among the Hellenistic marble scum
Glistens a vivid phallus; marsh-born here before
At a palm, cleft-suckled, a god he first came
Who hurts and heals unlike love, and whom I fear;
Will he return here? quickly we pluck dry flowers
The sailor blows his conch; Delos disappears

Mykonos

Brown bare island stretched to July sailing winds
At a beach houses blinding as snow; close-by
A warren of curved white walls; families within
Marine, the women, the girls are strict and shy;
On the saint's eve, the square where they danced was small
Like a Greek loft in New York; between candles, chairs
A slow row moved stocky in the night sea-chill
The saint's neighbors, the rest of the town not there;
In a bare room, like a sailor's few souvenirs
The sacred objects—vowed small church that mates build
Cold during winter—all-powerful Christ repairs
As Son to such a table and sweetness is fulfilled;
The rose like our blood in its perishable bloom
Sweetens with remembrance a white unlocked room

Ciampino
Envoi

Flying from Greece to see Moscow's dancing girl
I look down on Alba Longa, see Jacob's house
And the Pope's, and already the airplane's curls
Show St. Peter's, and the Appian tombs' remorse;
But Jacob, a two year old American
Is running in the garden in August delight;
"Forum not a park, Forum a woods," he opines
In November quiet there on days less bright;
Now in New York Jacob wants to have my cat
He goes to school, he behaves aggressively
He is three and a half, age makes us do that
And fifty years hence will he love Rome in place of me?
For with regret I leave the lovely world men made
Despite their bad character, their art is mild

Snoring in New York
An Elegy

When I come, who is here? voices were speaking
Voices had been speaking, lightly been mocking
As if in and out of me had been leaking
Three or four voices, falsely interlocking
And rising, one or two untruly falling
"When I come, who" screaming it or small calling

Let it call in the stinking stair going down
Mounting to a part, the topfloor ajar
On the subway, in the taxi, young and plain
Let it ring and roar, door and drawer, make and mar
The boys are not young boys, let them sit pretty
Out of habit, facing pity, no pity

Out of habit, a drying glazing of eyes
A crying habit streaking oblique the cheeks
The lips sucked as by weeping, the voices rise
Musically aping the howl of heartbreaks
Its loose head bobbing backward, body creeping
These voices, faces overhang my sleep

I slide from under and as through a twilight
Peer at noon over noon-incandescent sand
The wild-grown roses offer warbling delight
Smell of dwarf oaks, stunted pines wafts from the land
The grin of boys, the selfcentered smile of girls
Shines to my admiring the way a wave curls

Or just their eyes, stepping in washed cotton clothes
Tight or sheer, rubber and voile, in the city
Hot wind fanning the cement, if no one knows
Noon-incandescent, the feel at their beauty
Stranger's glance fondling their fleshed legs, their fleshed breast
They enjoy it like in a pierglass undressed

And enjoy the summer subway, bulge to bulge
The anonymous parts adhesive swaying
Massive as distortions that sleepers divulge
So in subterranean screeching, braying
Anaesthetizing roaring, over steel floors
Majestically inert, their langour flowers

And nude jump up joking alert to a date
Happy with the comb, the icebox, the car keys
How then if rings, phone or remark, their own fate
Fury, as unpersonal as a disease
Crushes graces, breaks faces, outside inside
Hirsute adults crying as fat babies cried

Covered over, lovered over and older
The utterance cracked and probing thievishly
Babyfied roving eye, secretive shoulder
The walk hoisted and drooped, exposed peevishly
The groom's, bride's either, reappears in careers
Looking fit, habitual, my dears, all these years

So at the opening, the ball, the spot abroad
At the all-night diner, the teen-age drugstore
Neighborhood bar, amusement park, house of God
They meet, they gossip, associate some more
And then commute, drive off, walk out, disappear
I open my eyes in the night and am here

Close them, safe abed, hoping for a sound sleep
Beyond the frontier that persons cross deranged
Anyone asleep is a trustful soft heap
But so sleeping, waking can be interchanged
You submit to the advances of madness
Eyes open, eyes shut, in anguish, in gladness

Through the windows in fragments hackies' speech drifts
Men, a whore, from the garage, Harlem or Queens
Call, dispute, leave, cabs finish, begin their shifts
Each throat's own pitch, fleshed, nervy or high, it leans
In my open ear, a New Yorker nearby
Moves off in the night as I motionless lie.

Summer New York, friends tonight at cottages
I lie motionless, a single retired man
White-haired, ferrety, feminine, religious
I look like a priest, a detective, a con
Nervously I step among the city crowd
My private life of no interest and allowed

Brutality and invisibility
We have for one another and to ourselves
Gossamer-like lifts the transparent city
Its levitating and ephemeral shelves
So shining, so bridged, so demolished a woof
Towers and holes we stand in that gales put to proof

Home of my free choice; drunk boys stomp a man who
Stared, girls encompass a meal ticket, hate fate
Like in a reformatory, what is true
To accept it is an act, to avoid it, great
New Yorkers shack up, include identify
Embrace me, familiarly smiling close-by

Opaque, large-faced, hairy, easy, unquiet
The undulant adolescents flow in, out
Pounce on a laugh, ownership, or a riot
The faces of the middle-aged, dropped or stout
But for unmotivatedness are like saint's
Hiding no gaps, admitting to all taints

They all think they look good—variegated
As aged, colored, beat—an air unsupported
But accustomed, corpulent more than mated
Young or old selfconsciousness uncomforted
Throw their weight—that they each do—nowhere they know
Like a baseball game, excessively fast, slow

Mythically slow or slow United States
Slow is not owned, not run, slow is like dearer
Two outside come to hear, one inside awaits
Mere fright at night, bright dismay by day, fear is
Wider, fear is nearly too close, small, no floor
Dear indoors is, fear is here and becomes more

More civilization; I have friends and you
Funny or evil in its selfimportance
Civilization people make for fun; few
Are anxious for it; though evil is immense
The way it comes and goes makes jokes; about love
Everybody laughs, laughs that there is enough

So much imagination that it does hurt
Here it comes, the irresistible creature
That the stars circle until one day they squirt
It lifts sunset-like abysses of feature
Sizes vertiginous, no place I can keep
Or will remember, leaping, falling asleep

"Out of Bronx subway June forest"

Out of Bronx subway June forest
A blue mallard drums the stream's reach
Duckling proud crosses lilyleaf
The thinnest of old people watch
And Brooklyn subway, Apt 5 J
Dozen young marvelous people
A painter's birthday, we're laughing
Real disaster is so near us
My joke on death they sweetly sink
Sunday follows, sleepy June rain
Delighted I carry icecream
A few blocks to friends' supper drenched
Baby with my name, old five weeks
I hold after its bath, it looks

"Old age, lookit, it's stupid, a big fart"

Old age, lookit, it's stupid, a big fart
Messy what you are, it's preposterous
Cane slips on the kerb, helped up, he grins, part
Apologetic, watchful, vain, a mess.
And the flash phantom jumps transparent jumps
Rust flange loose, eye walked with walking sweet bees
Straw coin, sky's green pin, own heart's shrewd lumps
Its submiss trees and ancient evasive ease.
Child's shrieks left tied in the dark who falls bruised
Like a senile man's squeaks of rage at chess
Girl's gorgeous, ten feet tall, smile unconfused
I'm a fool cared for, thank you yes, age, yes, such a mess.
Cat and kittens each summer my sweetheart
Consciousness shrinks, leaves them the larger part.

BARBARA GUEST

Barbara Guest was born in Wilmington, North Carolina in 1920. She grew up in California and Florida; she studied at UCLA, transferred to Berkeley, and then settled in New York in the early 1940s. There she became interested in the painting and writing of the Surrealists, which she has suggested was crucial to 'unlocking the kingdom of poetry' for many of her generation. Like Ashbery, O'Hara, and Schuyler, Guest was hired by Tom Hess to contribute reviews of the burgeoning New York art scene for *Art News*, and her early work reflects her conviction of the enormous aesthetic possibilities for poetry unleashed by the experiments of Abstract Expressionists such as Jackson Pollock, Willem de Kooning and Franz Kline. What most excited her about New York in this period was the sense that 'there was no recognized separation between the arts'. The painters' break with traditions of figuration led Guest to imagine a poetry that 'extended vertically, as well as horizontally', that refused to remain 'motionless within a linear structure'. Adopting the associative procedures of the Surrealists, she evolved a buoyant, haunting poetic language that foregrounded the processes of composition itself. Guest makes extensive use of techniques of collage; her extended lyrics such as 'The Farewell Stairway' or 'Blurred Edge' are tensile, airy structures in which fragmented narratives, moments of vision, and intense, painterly observations are played off against each other like themes within a symphony. Her work is insistently musical, and at its best radiates, to use her own phrase, 'a glowing impersonal empathy'. In this it resembles the abstract canvases of artists such as Grace Hartigan and Mary Abbott, with both of whom Guest has collaborated.

As well as over twenty-four volumes of poetry, Guest has published a novel, *Seeking Air* (1978), a highly acclaimed biography of H.D., *Herself Defined: The Poet H.D. and Her World* (1984), and a collection of essays, *Forces of the Imagination* (2003). Guest's poetry has not only been important to New York School writers, but has significantly influenced the work of a number of poets associated with Language writing. It was not, however, until towards the twilight of her career that Guest began to receive widespread recognition. Her 1989 collection, *Fair*

Realism, won the Lawrence Lipton Prize for Literature, and in 1999 she was awarded the Robert Frost Medal. Her work is increasingly being seen as a vital link between the modernism of H.D. and Virginia Woolf, and the avant-garde experiments in language of such as Fanny Howe and Ann Lauterbach. The last lines of this selection's final poem, drawn from her latest book, *The Red Gaze* (2005), aptly characterise her own achievement – 'filled with epiphany / night has known since infancy.'

Parachutes, My Love, Could Carry Us Higher

I just said I didn't know
And now you are holding me
In your arms,
How kind.
Parachutes, my love, could carry us higher.
Yet around the net I am floating
Pink and pale blue fish are caught in it,
They are beautiful,
But they are not good for eating.
Parachutes, my love, could carry us higher
Than this mid-air in which we tremble,
Having exercised our arms in swimming,
Now the suspension, you say,
Is exquisite. I do not know.
There is coral below the surface,
There is sand, and berries
Like pomegranates grow.
This wide net, I am treading water
Near it, bubbles are rising and salt
Drying on my lashes, yet I am no nearer
Air than water. I am closer to you
Than land and I am in a stranger ocean
Than I wished.

The Farewell Stairway

after Balla

The women without hesitancy began to descend
leaving flowers—

Ceres harried—bragged of cultivated grain—

I saw Hecate. the gray-wrapped woman.
in lumpy dark.

farewell eyes revolve—
the frontier oscillating—

pleated moments.
Hades at the bottom—

*

they laughed like twins their arms around each other
the women descending—

birds dropping south out of wind.

I thought there were many. goodbyes twisted
upwards from the neck—

tiny Arachne donating a web—

*

a common cloudy scene. no furniture.
a polished stairwell—

women magnetized. moving. chatting.

responding to the pull—

the vortex—

*

curves rapidly oscillating—

undulating to rapid pencil lines.

or water—

the look of stewed water.
sensuously.

and gnarled Charon—

*

their clothes—volumes—

folded over. blowing.
dresses approach the wide pencilling—

Hecate was present
and that other woman looking backward—

tearful. holding onto the rail.

I saw it futurally—

stoppered cotton slowly expanding. released.
sliding from the bottle—

*

I was outside the vortex. close to the wall.
Hecate managed me—

at the curve. the magic.
floated up—spiralled—

*

they were fully dressed. their volume.
the modish descent—

antiqueness—

*

a roman *scala.*

in the neighborhood of the *stazione.*

gli addii—gli addii—
velocity—

whipped the waves.

the vortex centered. reverent.

*

you who are outside. over there.
can't feel the pull. it makes you wonder—

the oscillation. the whirling. urgent.
indicating air revolving in a circuit—

without interruption. free movement
in *cielo puro*—spider-less—

scatters everything.

something overheard—beyond Lethe.
whispered—and the corollary—

*

diminuendo on the stair.
the slowed *salutando*—
flagrant barking from the shore—

keeping a stylish grip on themselves. serapes.

futurally extended.

*

south dusk and fire balls—

the same at Nauplia. mythic potency—

winding down the tower—

farewell. farewells.

Twilight Polka Dots

The lake was filled with distinguished fish purchased
at much expense in their prime. It was a curious lake,
half salt,
wishing to set a tone of solitude edged with poetry.
This was a conscious body aware of shelves and wandering
rootlings, duty suggested it provide a scenic atmosphere
of content, a solicitude for the brooding emotions.

It despised the fish who enriched the waters. Fish with their lithesome bodies, and their disagreeable concern with feeding. They disturbed the water which preferred the cultivated echoes of a hunting horn. Inside a mercantile heart the lake dwelt on boning and deboning, skin and sharpened eyes, a ritual search through dependable deposits for slimier luxuries. The surface presented an appeal to meditation and surcease.

Situated below the mountain, surrounded by aged trees, the lake offered a picture appealing both to young and mature romance. At last it was the visual choice of two figures who in the fixity of their shared glance were admired by the lake. Tactfully they ignored the lacustrine fish, their gaze faltered lightly on the lapping margins, their thoughts flew elsewhere, even beyond the loop of her twisted hair and the accent of his poised tie-pin.

The scene supplied them with theatre, it was an evening performance and the water understood and strained its source for bugling echoes and silvered laments. The couple referred to the lake without speech, by the turn of a head, a hand waved, they placed a dignity upon the lake brow causing an undercurrent of physical pleasure to shake the water.

Until the letter fell. Torn into fragments the man tossed it on the water, and the wind spilled the paper forward, the cypress bent, the mountain sent a glacial flake. Fish leapt. Polka dots now stippled the twilight water and a superannuated gleam like a browned autumnal stalk followed the couple where they shied in the lake marsh grass like two eels who were caught.

Dissonance Royal Traveller

sound opens sound

shank of globe   strings floating out

something like images are here

opening up avenues to view a dome

a distant clang reaches the edifice.

*

understanding what it means
to understand music

cloudless movement   beyond the neck's reach

an hypnotic lull in porcelain   water break   mimics

tonality   crunch of sand under waddling

a small seizure
from monumentality

does not come or go   with understanding

the path will end

birdhouse   of trembling cotton

or dream   expelled it
parcel   on the landlocked moor.

*

explaining music

and their clothes entangled

who walk into a puddle of minnows;

minnows in a bowl

consonant with water.

the drifted footpad

ambushed by reeds signals the listening

oars.

music disappears into oars.

*

in the middle the world is brown;
on the opposite side of the earth
an aroma of scarlet.

this accompanies our hearing music;
the sleeve of heaven
and the hoof of earth
loosed from their garrison.

dissonance may abandon *miserere*
on bruised knee hasten to the idol.

*

and what is consonance—the recluse—

entering and exiting
as often as a monarch butterfly
touches a season;

by accident grips the burning flowers.

in the stops between terror
the moon aflame on its plaza.

*

autumn of rippling wind
and the noise of baskets
smell of tin fists.

and harsh fists

on the waterfall changing the season;

the horse romps in flax

a cardboard feature

creating a cycle of flax.

music imagines this cardboard

the horse in cardboard jacket

flagrant the ragged grove

red summit red.

dissonance royal traveller

altered the red saddle.

Blurred Edge

It appears

a drama of   exacting dimension.

Anguished figure,

reign of terror.

Craft and above all

the object within.

Softness precedes

blurred edge.

A hint disappears   inside the earlier one.

*

<u>Softness still nudging.</u>

A different temperament,

inside an earlier plan.

Upon this stool is draped material
arabesque of an iron stool,

bare bones of the iron seat.

*

The arrangement of objects announced

more firmly than before.

Observation. Candor,

where candor approaches the cube.

Dark siphon bottle mood

of blurred edge.

*

Life permitted no privilege

no exegesis
no barnyard door. The feathered visage the domed hat

allowed no strange air or music.

An attempt to get beyond the arrangement,

the vibration of a peculiar touch.

*

It changes between eye and alarm,

the hibiscus,

more gifted.

Part of the tension,

is illusory.

*

A hint of what was going to be.

Covering and uncovering necessary.

Self pouring out of cloudedness.

If views of the lower body

do not conform,
a risk of being exposed,

Rain and altitude.

*

This is not sand, it is drama.

The anguished figure, sand blew away
that armor. A look extends the blur.

Other creatures alive,
word exchanged for meaning,
moment of descriptiveness.

Sand blows away

the carapace,
in the distance,
figure passing,
unworded distance at edge.

Outside of This, That Is

An oyster, the fragrance, greenleaf
floating dog outside and shuffle through hunger,
once again nothing so difficult when it passes in front as

December goes before the new year. A battalion
of festival largely in place by the region's devotion,
a flannel embrace, as if over, the green flavor.

A feathery existential bower shall block
the rude flagon. A grape
centennial passed
then passed as taught,
crowded by hope in a corral or anonymous
by the grape barrel, by the Ancients and
mixed the Novella with grievous
destiny.

A frame lets in elsewhere, a fairie
flies through Bretagne, or guessed she flew,
Romance let her in. Others walk outside,
plants that wait their copying into the future,
that is.

Nostalgia of the Infinite

after Giorgio de Chirico, 1913

Hands are touching.
You began in cement in small spaces.
You began the departure. Leaves restrain. You attempted the departure.
A smile in sunshine, nostalgia.

I have lost my detachment, sparrow with silver teeth.
I have lost the doves of Milan, floating politely.

Recognize me, I shall be here, O Nietzsche.
We have skipped down three pairs of stairs,
they are not numbered, they are oddly assorted, velvet.

Recognize me in sunshine.
Bulletins permit us to be freer than in Rome.
Castles perched on a cliff.
Filled with pears and magic.

I am not detached,
bulletins permit us comb, fish of silver.
A part of the tower
beckons to us.

The Hungry Knight

Palest shadow on the middle rock,

Hungry Knight! drifting.

O causes,

O celebrants,

massive,

comfort had ceased.

Massive night falls on the middle rock,

weighing-in like a scholar.

Heavy is the literature

bred on the rock,

filled with epiphany

night has known since infancy.

Kenward Elmslie

Kenward Elmslie was born in New York City in 1929. His father was a British businessman, and his mother, Constance Pulitzer, the daughter of the newspaper magnate Joseph Pulitzer. He has described himself as of Scottish-Irish-English-Hungarian-Jewish-German descent. His early childhood was spent in Colorado Springs, Colorado; he later attended schools in Washington DC, Virginia, Ohio, and Massachusetts, and went on to study literature at Harvard, where he overlapped with (but barely knew at the time) Koch, Ashbery, and O'Hara, graduating in 1950. He moved to Cleveland and began writing song lyrics, becoming a librettist of lyric theatre (musicals, operas and eventually cabaret). He collaborated with Ned Rorem on an adaptation of Strindberg's *Miss Julie* performed in 1965 by the New York City Opera, who that same year presented his version of the life of the murderess Lizzie Borden, for which Jack Beeson composed the music. Other adaptations include Chekhov's *The Seagull* and *The Three Sisters*, Henry James's *Washington Square* and Truman Capote's *The Grass Harp*, for which he composed the book and lyrics. In the 1970s he began devising texts such as 'Girl Machine' (included here), for performance artists. These he occasionally performs himself, wearing a specially designed hat that resembles an outsized brassière. Elmslie began sending out fiction and poetry to little magazines in the mid-1950s; his first collection of poetry, *Pavilions*, was published by Tibor de Nagy Editions in 1961. Elmslie has also frequently collaborated with painters, in particular his partner of thirty years, Joe Brainard, who died in 1994. And Elmslie has done much to promote the work of numerous writers associated with the New York School: his Z Press and *Z Magazine* has published the work of John Ashbery, Bill Berkson, Harry Mathews, Ron Padgett, James Schuyler, Anne Waldman and Marjorie Welish, among others.

John Ashbery has described the voice that speaks much of Elmslie's poetry as like that 'of a mad scientist who has swallowed the wrong potion in his lab and is desperately trying to get his calculations on paper before everything closes in'. There is a strongly performative dimension to Elmslie's antic humour; his poems hurtle forward with the manic energy of a Looney Tunes cartoon, but seem always conscious of their own artificiality, of the need not to look down and see they are running on thin air. The more garish his landscapes and zany his characters, however, the more one grows aware of the 'bare bones', to borrow the title of his moving elegy for Joe Brainard, that lurk beneath, and which seem to motivate his restless pageants of invention and surprise.

Experts at Veneers

"In Montana, claws skim through the dawn,
herders just saddle up, yes that's it!
But then, they gulp hiccough pills in the highschools,
not to skip one ambiance in the tunnel of fun."

That symbiosis in the garden says to adventure.
The jelly on the daffodil will mildew by July,
and the orange result if the birds come by
will suffice as our capitol, won't it?
    And I was there, and I was there.

Here we are, in what seems to be an aerial predicament,
The Government certainly looks handsome in the mackerel sky,
awaiting wind fungus, beribboned in *its* way, goodbye.
Blackamoor stump, how luminous you'll be.
    And I was there, and I was there.

History of France

Wind, cold, rain.
Then came the sky person:
a pale empress.

Today is beautiful—
such lively girls!
A sharp-cornered stone hovers.

Ah, rigid acceptance!
Money buys everything
except walls between people.

The empire in the rain
with the muzzled atmosphere
stopped us at the border.

Striped barriers! Oafs!
And beyond, men in swimsuits shout,
"Art, make us free."

Another plaintive morning
full of chickens, dust, and buoys.
The sea keeps re-beginning . . .

Lobster claws in the pine forests
betoken an illogical sea
which sings: I *know*, I *know*.

Sticky tar and plastic messes
clarify the alliance of judge and guide.
True democracy need never exist.

Not only need, but never will.
Think of cliffs. Think of peacocks.
And the salty skiffs of the colonels.

Withdrawing rooms come next—perfumed earphones
for the young people: it's the Divine Sarah.
Wooden leg sounds bump about the divans.

"Secrecy in the provinces,
a journey under a waterfall—
these won't test your manhood, Robert."

A pretty woodwind, and thrushes.
They say the dormers fly open
to admit sweet-faced aristocrats.

And the maids dump out the cakes,
the pretty bush designs on the main course,
while everyone hides letters in hollow trees.

The party includes the lady with the map-shaped face,
the boyish man, the chess-playing lifeguard;
how they love the French summers recently.

The cleverer towns have crested yellow parks,
nice and oblong with ferns and pebble deer,
and on these the old sweet lovers loll (the wasps).

Underneath them, musical flushing,
tunnels to the ocean,
and bloated hairy sea creatures.

We have never (bump) sat on (bump) rocks,
the women facing west,
and watched the Atlantic and Pacific sunset,

the men tucked into blankets,
the children tucked in too,
and the old people in the cars.

Well done! You see, the cities
have erected spangled circus nets
or are they nests?

Into them (keep whirring, pap factories)
ocean souvenirs fall, misty bitchy things,
so the boulevards get more usage.

Now, in the mountain gravel pits,
the workers wear scoopy hats,
in which they smuggle out the granules.

But in the mauve valleys,
such attractive colleges.
All built on animal cemeteries, alas.

In winter, they pack 'em solid,
come spring, to Hans and Ivan's amazement,
but now—he reaches the valuables:

fountains of exposed beasts and breasts,
lottery tickets in the sluices,
to prevent the acids from seeping through.

In the warehouses, racketeers
daydream of that shy person,
the pale empress.

At lunchtime, they take it out,
the tongue-shaped wooden box;
today is beautiful.

Shirley Temple Surrounded by Lions

In a world where kapok on a sidewalk looks like an "accident"
—innards—would that freckles could enlarge, well, meaningfully
into kind of friendly brown kingdoms, all isolate,
with a hero's route, feral glens,
and a fountain where heroines cool their mouths.

Scenario: an albino industrialiste, invited to the beach at noon
(and to such old exiles, oceans hardly teem with ambiguities)
by a lifeguard after her formulae, though in love—
"Prop-men, the gardenias, the mimosa need anti-droopage stuffing."
Interestingly slow, the bush and rush filming.

Hiatus, everyone. After the idea of California sort of took root,
we found ourselves in this cookie forest; she closed the newspaper,
groped past cabanas, blanched and ungainly.
The grips watched Marv and Herm movies of birds tweeting,
fluttering around and in and out an old boat fridge, on a reef,
when eek, the door—or was it "eef"—"Shirl" said the starling, end of—

The janitors are watching movies of men and women ruminating.
Then a cartoon of two clocks, licking. Chime. Licking, chime. *Then a* ?
After that, photos of incinerators in use moved families more than
the candy grass toy that retches. Dogs. For the dressers, "Mutations",
about various feelers. For the extras, movies of revenge that last.

This spree *has to* last. "Accept my pink eyes, continual swathing",
Shirley rehearsed. "Encase me in sand, then let's get kissy".
Do children have integrity, i.e. eyes ? Newsreels, ponder this.
How slow the filming is for a grayish day with its bonnet
bumping along the pioneer footpath, pulled by—here, yowly hound.

Japanese City

Centennial of Melville's birth this morning.
Whale balloons drift up released by priests. Whale Boats parade
followed by boats of boys in sou'westers jiggled by runners
followed by aldermen in a ritual skiff propelled by "surf"—girls.
In my hotel room with its cellophane partitions (underwatery)
I phone down for ice-water, glass, tumbler, and the cubes.

Cattle for the Xmas Market fill the streets.
Black snouts—a rubby day indeed. Bump the buildings, herds.
A Mexican seamstress brings back my underthings shyly
six, seven times a day. One sweats so, lying about.
She mentions marvelous pistachio green caverns
where one canoes through cool midgy Buddha beards

where drafts of polar air sound like cicadas, where—
About the partitions. The other travellers seem—
There were beautiful hairs in the wash-basin this A.M.—
thick, and they smelled of limes
(good, that jibes with mine—ugh!—)
but mine, how perverse! Form a hoop, you there. Mine,

mine smell like old apples in a drawer. Jim the Salesman
and his cohorts are massaging my feet—a real treadmill example.
They're in lawn decor, ether machines, and nocturnal learning clasps.
And Jim? Plays cards in his shorts, moves black fish around.
Black houses, the capitol. Hotel chunks. Sky chunks. The squeeze:
green odd numbers—white air, amputations and eagles, respite.

Red even numbers—body sections, the ocean sac, the great beach.
Green even numbers—oval jewels, quicksand, the haven behind the falls.
Jim's stammer is contagious, zen smut about hatcheries in the suburbs,
how the women in the canneries came down with the "gills,"
hence bathtub love-makings, couplings in the sewers. The ice-water comes.

The room-clerk's pate shines up through the transparent floor.
Soon the sin couples will start arriving, and the one-way mirror teams
and the government professionals with their portable amulets—
shiny vinyl instruments that probe and stretch.
Much visiting back and forth. Pink blobs. Revels and surveys.
Many olive eyes'll close in a sleep of exhaustion. More ice-water!

The celebrants in metal regalia jangle and tinkle
moving past the red-roofed villas of the Generals,
past the cubicles of the nakeds and into the harbor,
past the glum stone busts of the Generals, sitting in the water.
Out they go, (Jim etc.) into the sweet emptied city, leaving behind
the red odd numbers untouched: pleasure beaches, monsoons and sun.

Feathered Dancers

Inside the lunchroom the travelling nuns wove
sleeping babies on doilies of lace.
A lovely recluse jabbered of bird lore and love:
"Sunlight tints my face

and warms the eggs outside
perched on filthy columns of guilt.
In the matted shadows where I hide,
buzzards moult and weeds wilt."

Which reminds me of Mozambique
in that movie where blacks massacre Arabs.
The airport runway (the plane never lands, skims off) is bleak—
scarred syphilitic landscape—crater-sized scabs—

painted over with Pepsi ads—
as in my lunar Sahara dream—giant net comes out of sky,
encloses my open touring car. Joe slumps against Dad's
emergency wheel turner. Everyone's mouth-roof dry.

One interpretation. Mother hated blood!
When the duck Dad shot dripped on her leatherette lap-robe,
dark spots not unlike Georgia up-country mud,
her thumb and forefinger tightened (karma?) on my ear-lobe.

Another interpretation. Motor of my heart stalled!
I've heard truckers stick ping-pong balls up their butt
and jounce along having coast-to-coast orgasms, so-called.
Fermés, tousled jardins du Far West, I was taught—tight shut.

So you can't blame them. Take heed, turnpikes.
Wedgies float back from reefs made of jeeps: more offshore debris.
Wadded chewy depressants and elatants gum up footpaths. Remember Ike's
"Doctor-the-pump-and-away-we-jump" Aloha Speech to the Teamsters? "The—"

he began and the platform collapsed, tipping him onto a traffic island.
An aroused citizenry fanned out through the factories that day
to expose the Big Cheese behind the sortie. Tanned,
I set sail for the coast, down the Erie and away,

and ate a big cheese in a café by the docks,
and pictured every room I'd ever slept in:
toilets and phone-calls and oceans. Big rocks
were being loaded, just the color of my skin,

and I've been travelling ever since,
so let's go find an open glade,
like the ones in sporting prints,
(betrayed, delayed, afraid)

where we'll lie among the air-plants
in a perfect amphitheatre in a soft pink afterglow.
How those handsome birds can prance,
ah . . . unattainable tableau.

Let's scratch the ground clean,
remove all stones and trash,
I mean open dance-halls in the forest, I mean
where the earth's packed smooth and hard. Crash!

It's the Tale of the Creation. The whip cracks.
Albatrosses settle on swaying weeds.
Outside the lunchroom, tufts and air-sacs
swell to the size of fruits bursting with seeds.

Circus Nerves and Worries

When that everybody's legal twin Mrs Trio
enters the casino, I expect personal disaster.
Out of next winter's worst blizzard I'm convinced
into the lobby and up the ladder she'll hustle
holding that squeaky velvet purse to one ear.
Placing one green and black peppermint-striped chip
gingerly on zero, zero it is. Which is when I fall dead.
In my shower while soaping. This very next year.

Goony intuition? Well, once in April at the Café Jolie
pointblank she asked, this terror at time in your eyes,
wouldn't crossing a river help? How about now?
Give up my innocence hunt, I exclaimed,
intimacies with failure, all my "sudden magic" hopes?
And today came this dream about moths, I lied,
mouthing, yes wisdoms. Only how to read their lips?
   Tell me! Tell me!
I dream about vines, she said. Thank you and ciao.

Yesterday I looked at my body. Fairly white.
Today fairly white, the same. No betterment.
Why can't I feel air ? Or take in mountains?
I lose my temper at pine needles, such small stabs.
Breezes scratch me (different from feeling)
and I long to breathe water. Agenda tomorrow:
Cable her care of casino TIME TERROR GONE
STOP SEAWEED DREAM GREAT STOP (actually,
   a lie)

Girl Machine

my nerves   my nerves   I'm going mad
my nerves   my nerves   I'm going mad
round-the-world
hook-ups
head lit up   head lit up   head lit up
the fitting   the poodle
MGM MGM MGM
MGM MGM MGM
MGM MGM MGM
the fitting   the poodle

What a life just falling in and out of
What a life just falling in and out of
swimming pools
xylophones   WANTED   xylophones
WANTED   female singer   WANTED
bigtime floorshow   bigtime floorshow
bigtime floorshow   bigtime floorshow

Busby Berkeley
silhouetted in moonlight moonlight
silhouetted in moonlight moonlight
mysterious mirrors
mysterious mirrors
Gold Diggers of Bllankety Blank
Clickety Clack   Clickety Clack
swell teeth   not news
swell teeth   not news
woo-woo   woo-woo
woo-woo   woo-woo
Gold Diggers of Blankety Blank
Gold Diggers of Blankety Blank
Clickety Clack   Clickety Clack

shiny black surfaces
shiny black surfaces
shiny black surfaces

a girl machine
a girl machine

work work work   work work work
work work work   work work work
work work work   work work work
work work work work work

show gets on and is a smasheroo
show gets on and is a smasheroo
round-the world
hook-ups

Busby Berkeley is the Albert Einstein
of the movie mu
Quantum Leap
Babe Rainbow
Girl Machine   Girl Machine
Quantum Leap
Babe Rainbow
Girl Machine   Girl Machine

reflected and refracted
by black floors and mystery meers
black floors and mystery meers

Night in Shanghai
Night in Shanghai
Girl Machine   Girl Machine
Girl Machine   Girl Machine

lips painted red
Girl Machine   Girl Machine
Girl Machine   Girl Machine
keep on doing it
the oriental fans part

Girl Machine   Girl Machine
Girl Machine   Girl Machine
distant hands

Girl Machine   Girl Machine
Girl Machine   Girl Machine
they come nearer

Girl Machine   Girl Machine
Girl Machine   Girl Machine
pursued by gangs

down a shadowy dream corridor
Girl Machine   Girl Machine
Girl Machine   Girl Machine
they get smaller

a shadowy endless dream corridor
Girl Machine   Girl Machine
Girl Machine   Girl Machine
distant hands

Girl Machine   Girl Machine
Girl Machine   Girl Machine
down a shadowy endless dream corridor
the oriental fans close

42nd St   42nd St   42nd St   42nd St
42nd St   42nd St   42nd St   42nd St
reflected and refracted
by black floors and mystery meers
42nd St   42nd St   42nd St   42nd St
42nd St   42nd St   42nd St   42nd St
black floors and mystery meers

you in the view
and no real walls
you in the view
and no real walls

firm shiny terror
express flow
black whi

you in the view
and no real walls
you in the view
and no real walls

Girl Machine Girl Machine
Girl Machine Girl Machine
Girl Machine Girl Machine
Girl Machine Girl Machine
Girl Machine Girl Machine
Girl Machine Girl Machine

bunches like flowers
down the ramp
beautiful people working for us

Girl Machine Girl Machine
Girl Machine Girl Machine
Girl Machine Girl Machine
Girl Machine Girl Machine

happy factory
just relax

Girl Machine Girl Machine
Girl Machine Girl Machine
Girl Machine Girl Machine
Girl Machine Girl Machine

just relax
just relax

just

relax

relax

Diddly Squat
From Cyberspace

Motor mouth overflow has tapered off. I head home. Dish with CW how
Wayne's a wife-beater.
Carlos asks Ruth for a blow job. She tells him direct approach a turn-off.
Prefers Romance.
Derek has white-streaked hair now, looks old. In Paris, we ordered *vin ordinaire*
by the litre.
At the funeral, his step-bro Chuck spreads the word, Derek has ants in his
asshole pants.

I move to a new megalopolis. Hyperactive child asks me, "Who's *your* guru,
bozo?"
Obligatory Q & A, pro or con *Marrow Gobs,* imposter-surgeon infrastructure
skinflick.
Same day impromptu wave to Alan funicular to the morgue. He struck raffish
pose. So?
No dhow float for Untouchables Triathlon, fund flush toilets in sister city's jinrik-

isha depots. *Jeunesse dorée* survival guilt. At two, I knew to let Sancerre breathe.
At four, special abattoir solved the foie gras conundrum. By ten, anus force-fed
brains
a no-no after sunset, in labyrinthine sex warrens crumbling under the aban-
doned wreath
of wealth rotunda. Long since ceased and desisted live whistle blowing. Plenty
else profanes

the air I subsist on, the cocoon I curl up in to make ready for the morrow.
April, my birth month, flashed by quicker'n a chicken pursued by a musical
saw robot.
After her life-affirmative mink stole punch-line, my surrogate, Missy Sorrow,
'll shroud herself and prance airily up the gangplank into the showboat.

Doing OK, scouting for shards. Forgot ancestral magnifying glass under my
hankies,
condoms, sox (don't always match, ribs diverge). I'm used to my bureau's
muss
and I don't miss prisms unseen. Yesterday, under an assortment of dank keys,
came across a words-bunched-up epistle ending *"keepyourfilthyeuros"* plus

an unfinished PS: *"ifyoubalanceonevernaleggina"* — signed Victor. Knock Knock, Victor, whoever you were. In a *what?* Eidolon? *Passez-moi* some watermelon rind. Ygg, my creation myth, still engorges Tom Courtney and his variegated ilk. Shock of recognition has petered out. Ruts and more ruts. Hurdy-gurdy a plus, sky a find.

Bare Bones

It was love at first sight on the Staten Island ferry.

I'm part of an anti-Nam Poet Protest he and Ted Berrigan come to.

We collaborate. He artist, me words. Me, poet-librettist reduced to comic strip balloons? It's a ruse, to be with him.

He has his weird side. Two shrimp cocktails—that's his main course.

Our first tennis date. Interrogated closely, he assures me he plays well. He can't even hit the ball. I curse my luck. I've fallen for a dysfunctional mythomaniac.

We undress. His mysterious undergarment fascinates and scares me. It hangs loose from his bony arms, skinny torso, the hunchy back he's so ashamed of. Raggedy yellow loops. Waif Macramé. Dleam Come Tlue. My Very Own Urchin Savant. Only he isn't mine.

Triangle. Jealous anguish. Oh, the searing yearning. I put my foot down. Triangle tapers off, sort of. Gray area. Nights off.

He's late for dinner. I probe, against our code. He explains, innocent of the merest shred of guilt, surprise outside sex plus small talk takes time. High ground fury, nowhere to go. Chastened, I heat up the meal. We eat. In bed, we share Champale.

He's big on holidays. All holidays. Even Groundhog Day. A-Day stands for our Anniversary Day—our first night. Holidays mean gifts. His core belief, Gypsy source: Be Rememberethéd For What Thou Givest, Seeking Nothing Back. Except the pleasure giving gives.

He raises gift-giving to a noble art, as finely honed, as viewer-friendly as—his Art.

He gives me The Dolly Sisters in pastel sailor drag: Art Deco statuette. I'm appalled. Initially. Slowly he teaches me to give up received "good taste."

His recurrent dream. Finding jewels, buried jewels. We begin exchanging rings. Every Xmas. Birthdays.

He makes me necklace collages. Charms. Enamels. A cluster, minuscule photos of him, in miniature glass lockets with glass fronts—his face and naked body parts. Surefire way to get touched at parties, he points out. As if the gift weren't enough.

He stutters. Low voice. Can't make out his words. Bend close. Tulsa accent. E becomes I. Pinitintiary. Pass me the pin. Pen, Joe. Pen.

I hand him wine-lists, so I can hear him wrap his stutter around Pouilly-Fuissé. His spelling is a hoot. Phonetic printed Block Upper Case. I'm his checker, see his writings first, thrilling perk. His mental geography maps are surreal. Australia is in Europe,Venice its capital.

Europe honeymoon. Spoleto Poetry Fest. Rome airport. I panic. Train sked, how, *stazione* where? My sensible beloved rescuer cuts through the problem. Taxi.

Taxi. From Rome Airport to Spoleto. Subsequently from Madrid to Granada. Subsequently everywhere in foreign lands.

Pre-Armani, he hates jackets and ties, wears jeans, white shirt unbuttoned way down to reveal his chest mat. So teen-age cute, Spoleto impresario Gian-Carlo Menotti takes me aside. *Festivale Duo Mondo*! Spender! Yevtushenko! Ezra Pound! Hustlers are a no-no! Explain he's a genius? Flash our first collab, *The Baby Book?* Quote blurbs from obliging chums?

Frank O'Hara: *"The most peculiar thing I've ever read."*

Andy Warhol: *"FAN-tastic. FAN-tastic."*

Ron Padgett: *"The Greatest Book Of All Time.."*

I dummy up. *Ciao* Spoleto.

Our M.O. evolves. Four months together in Vermont, June to October, under the same roof. Rest of the year, delicate but tenacious bonds. Time off. We cohere, summer to summer, despite caesuras, rifts and dumpings, one each, luckily staggered.

In hosp, he mentions we've lasted thirty-one years.

In hosp, he says he thinks of us as married.

In hosp, he says I'm doing better than he expected, dealing with the circles of hell he's descending deeper and deeper into.

In hosp, he says we've been faithful. We've had a good life.

Proud moment. We're at Naropa. Allen beseeches, cheer up poor old lonely old Wm Burroughs. Dead flesh eyes don't waste a sec on me, sparkle. Reptilian lust. Allen: "Bill, they're a couple."

Bad times. His new lover, wily dominatrix, sneaks up on us both. Speed.

Thirty-something, I swell, take dex. Share fifty-fifty this Ted drug he's used since his Tulsa teens. Blissful bond, enabling dex togetherness. How brilliantly he works, long hours a snap.

Esthetic micro-management other artists would kill for. Protean quantity, star quality, as his last one-man smash proves.

I cross the abyss. His city studio is a madhouse of mounds, red here, yellow there, color-coded raw material screaming—

COLLAGE ME! COLLAGE ME! Turn me into jewels!

I partake of the white powder, his lover. We try to collab. The Way We Were. Nada. Nada. It's the black pit. I flee.

He comes out of it on his own. Wishy-washy, not all there, summer in Vermont, he cleans his brushes, tries to make art, settles for non-stop reading. His fave—Barbara Pym.

He-as-artist rematerializes fully, once. For me. *Sung Sex* drawings. Boy-in-bed odalisques. Japanesey abstractions. Lola, my cat, whose Fancy Feast he fluffs up mornings first thing.

He holds these drawings in low esteem, tiptoes away from the casino paradise: Art Biz gulag. Closes shop.

Despite snake-oil panaceas, his hair recedes. Small bald spot I can't get enough of. Older eyes, still kid thin.

Quel horreur! His face turns into Nixon, one visual he must never never know of.

He loves to see old couples hold hands, worries how The Young, purple hair, pierced flesh, must terrify The Old.

June '93. I have diabetes.My new better half takes charge. No nonsense trainer, genteel carer, patient restorer, he walks me, pushes me further, further. Drop 40 pounds by summer's end. Sugar plummets to normal. End of No Win.

Which I should've been prepared for. He always comes through, makes the best of a crisis situation. When Jimmy S uproots beds of day lilies, starts washing money in my kitchen sink, J.A. (hapless Vt. guest) and spit-prone I turn into Joan Crawford parodies, wide-eyed at full-moon psychopath clomping up the cliff-house stairwell. He takes command, talks Jimmy S into the waiting police car.

The first plague death. Bill Elliott. Super-cute. So-o-o nice. Ex of his, song collaborator-gig-pianist-crush of mine.

I bring up lovemaking: death risk. I think I'm thinking of my own survival. What I don't dare think is unwittingly being the instrument of his death. We become companionate.

Test. I'm OK. Privacy transgression. I ask. He's OK.

Flash forward. He tells me he has AIDS. In Vermont, he can't tan. The sun is lethal.

What I've always wanted happens. He takes care of me more, shoulders more of the domestic round. We take care of each other. A balance achieved, we're content together.

His insides act up. He goes to hosp, comes back too weak for walks. Our last October. We discuss our respective deaths. Ashes commingled, field uphill. Us both.

In NYC, all fall and winter and spring, he weakens.

On May 25th, late afternoon, he dies.

By a white quartz boulder, encircled by pines, field up-hill, I scatter Joe Brainard's ashes. Flesh ash, bone ash.

Promise kept. Closure.

Remembrance.

Venus Preserved

sloshy sounds and high wire maneuvers
from gondola to worn stones as cold
as old holy toes
smoothed by Crusader kisses

step out I'm lost
easy satori
of labyrinth aimlessness
jigsaw pink walls and water
fat sun sinks
garlic mayo glistens

crane at fancy dress doges
courtesans with perky-eared lap dogs
that stumblebum's Gregory Corso

wallet gone
light-fingered charm boy
leaves me my passport

get measured for gig
off-white silk pajamas

me-as-Oscar
Wilde exiled

Harry Mathews

Harry Mathews was born in 1930 on the Upper East Side of New York City, where he grew up. He studied music at Princeton and Harvard, and conducting in Paris in the early 1950s. In 1954 he moved with his first wife, the artist Niki de Saint Phalle, to Deiá, Mallorca, home of Robert Graves, whose *The White Goddess* had some influence on Mathews's first novel, *The Conversions* (1962). Soon after his return to Paris in 1956 he met John Ashbery, recently arrived on a Fulbright scholarship. Ashbery's poetry and ideas about literature made a deep impression on Mathews. In 1961 they began editing, along with the New York-based James Schuyler and Kenneth Koch, the magazine *Locus Solus*, named after the second novel of one of Ashbery and Mathews's great heroes, Raymond Roussel. Although only four issues of the magazine were published, it played an important role in assembling and printing – often for the first time – the work of many of the poets featured in this volume.

Mathews is probably better known for his fiction than his poetry. Novels such as *Cigarettes* (1987) and *The Journalist* (1994), and the short stories collected in *The Human Country* (2002), have made him one of America's most highly esteemed prose stylists. He was the first American to become a member of the Oulipo (Ouvroir de Littérature Potentielle), a Paris-based group of writers that included Raymond Queneau, Georges Perec and Italo Calvino, dedicated to exploring the literary possibilities of arbitrary constraints and mathematical formulae. His poetry is occasionally composed within restrictive, Oulipian forms, but he also shares with the Ashbery of *The Tennis Court Oath* an interest in drastic reworkings of genres, as for instance in his explosive fragmentation of the pastoral in 'Comatas'. Although based for much of his life in France (in Paris and in Lans-en-Vercors, in the French pre-Alps) Mathews's poetry illustrates many of the techniques and ideals of poets associated with the New York School. This is not surprising given his friendships with Ashbery, with Schuyler and with Kenneth Koch, who inspired the last poem in this selection, 'Lateral Disregard'. Its opening line, 'Shall I compare thee to a summer's bay', typifies Mathews's delight in irreverent word-play, in distortions of the familiar that then release an unforeseen set of linguistic patterns and associations. Like his fiction, Mathews's poetry often seems to proceed according to some inscrutable hidden law that keeps just eluding one's grasp. His fracturing of syntax and insistent melding of the concrete and abstract infuse his poetic landscapes with a haunting mixture of the fantastic and actual. The best of his poems brilliantly succeed in creating what Marianne Moore – an early enthusiasm – once called 'imaginary gardens with real toads in them'.

The Relics

THE DEVOTED SPY

Where are the brass islands?
There are the brass islands.
Their yellow wheat does not bend, and their peaks
Ring, flat. Their brass ports
Have a stupid glory in thin dusk—
By day, even near-yellow scrap copper
In that drab gold is sweet relief.
Streets are stiff with the wink and clink
Of wired lids, a deaf clatter
Of brass feet that batter brass,
Brass teeth, brass tears,
Brass breasts! In one such city
I found a mop of red rags
But left, my business done. I forget
The color. It is dazzling here to see poppies—
Wild poppies salt the harvest wheat
Like memorial ribbons red among tubas.

THE BATTLE

The sun rose red as parsley
And several ill-sewn drums
Ejected clouds of fish through the grass
Whose nostrils drew a wild smoke.
Beyond was a beach of gunpowder (beautiful:
Its bones small but barbed), but neither
I nor the water could reach it, and gulls
Fell along it with soft harassed explosions
That left lemon-smell and a sound of triangles
In the air, on the bones a whitish moisture.
Sweet things! A few cigarettes
Brought a dozen round, which I assembled
In a matter of years, despite their barbs
And soapishness; and the machine talked
Nonsense, and was uneatable. I decided
To desert, applying the wit left me
To become an amateur bomb, and jump

—With some anxiety, for the sea was swarming—
Onto the beach. I arose successful
A sad vibration of tuning forks
To touch some colors, wines, moons,
And laundry boiling in wintriness.

DAFFODILS, OR THEODORA'S TRAIN

They built the basilica on battered bones and bombed it.
Then it was. Relics and their guards became
A vague dust over puzzled mosaics;
But it is. I miss the pink-eared angels,
And the heartfelt noise of harmoniums at dusk
Interwoven with caterwauls; the garden too
Is grime where the earth fluttered with tearbanes,
Fustre, elgue, and tender paperdews
Sweetening the souls of hot cigars:
Yet why mourn?
The strand is merged mud, shadeless,
Undrying; I eat lost eels and fatigued
Field-snakes; my body's my only company,
But the world is whole. When over the ocean
Ashes regretful loom and unfurl
Towards land and evening, the sun flattens them.
I parody dead astronomers who extracted
Dead stars from their slaty wills,
My hands reaping light where black
Ooze divulges her yellow tesserae.

Invitation to a Sabbath

Rales of Easter . . . The sucking . . .
The ghastly gaiety of returning strangers
Inspired a vacuum of enormous tenuity.
There came (it was a day when cracked
Boy was found in a furrow drain,
Naked, smelling of heavenly smoke,
Chanting red places, cakes, tits,
Wings) a liquescent company, eight
Ladies in plaids among the disbanding mercury,
Four cavaliers in secular chasubles.
Vanished, vanished—
Their milky exhausts, gathered in tearbottles
Of perilous alabaster, illuminate nothing
Made thick: the ash tree stands in the stars.

Spell

The annunciation of time harrying time
Love.   The train rattles shrewdly.   Fail

Everlasting
Allpowerful, allbeloved
Invoked as sumptuary princess to a necessitous moon
Intromission and power
Elegance, heaven, and therapy enliven this throb
Here pleasure and coolness deepen as a mirror, if I were you
Nuts! a patter; boys and girls singing, time dragging us through a tight barricade of grapes popping
Zones of confusion, adoration—are we to look up again
And within us and without us the stale bathwaters of Capri
Io answers the zenith's inadequate lure
Here and after, return, return, hands, yellow implosions! I
Lie. The spirit hangs against the barracks.
Lead to . . . as if traffics were furnished to time
Brewed rife, ignited gossamer, in triumph triumph's essay
        The Passover riot calculated by the dim

(Emerald, and yellow)
Alders and warts postfigure the bloods, the blood of the connivers

Severance,
Prism of their mutable raj

The Sense of Responsibility

The society in my head
Said the viper in the washrag
Having no creator, requires my love:
"Eton pets who lag in their Latin
At a slow trot, who become of note
Reversing their school-step (as the apple ate Adam),"—
Divination without divinity
Affirmed the viper in the twirled spaghetti
Morse-tusks clatter in paleocrystic seas
My absurd blood is thin chrism
For my creatures by default, the default not mine:
I trace the reversions of their secular swarm.

Comatas

In the snowy yard a baroque thermometer,
Its foot freezing my pale fig-face
In its quicksilver bell, marks zero
On the china backing with a stripe of blue,
Whose top, scalloped as a cipher for waves,
The legend *Océan Atlantique* explains,
For the stripe (which the mercury glass bisects)
Separates *Père Europe* on the left
And Centigrade side from *Notre Fille*
L'Amérique, the Fahrenheit column. Yet the continents
Are not mere persons: dun elevator-shafts
Mount the parallel gradations, bucolic

In their details—Silenus asleep in the mezzanine
Of Europe, Arcadians in blue jeans on either
Third floor competing transatlantically,
A marsh of nymphs above one, a hive
Of wild bees on the shaft's wall,
The upper floors empty but for a woodland
Mist or smoke through which a woman
Yellow-haired and slim is vaguely naked
On the right—is it for her one wants to
Test the cedar elevator-boxes
That rise with the disintegration of icicles and lace?
If we entered, I must do so in exile and imagine
America (and you, my remembrance) opposite
Through tiered nature zooming towards innocence
Numbered dream of parallel transcendence
Perhaps?
                    your hair muddles
The real and the false in such ambitious copulation
That touching between our straining souls
Each skin with nerveless amorous indifference
Our minds are debauched, and our bodies are balloons—
        "The little girls—sighs of tar
        I'th'giddy wheat. On hieratic mountains
        I raped the bright corpses of daemons,
        Tractors shuttling yellowly below.
        O valleys. I examine my exact feet
        By Proust. Ladies, have a drink—shadows
        Wander in through your children, and swallows
        Spin quietly in the tender air."

And now before us the snows are stretched
Still and all the (look!) air's
Gusty music thins; may honeys
Run for him. The ripple of her ribs
Flash like the Var where the bullocks drink
And woven ferns droop from the bank
—In the shade I dream that my quiet singing
Mixes that beauty with itself; and a shadow
Of crows or nymphs speckles the field.

Jack This one-eared Negro walks round the world in a step
Jacques This one-eyed Indian's happy when he cries in the dark
Jack If A follows B, and I you, find "me"

Jacques If you're after me—who are you?
Jack How can a hard sleeper sleep with the light on?
Jacques (They bore me to death with their broad vowels!)
Jack When was she not a cunning stunt?

the tense of her tendons

Soon he was ware of a spring, in a hollow land, and the rushes grew thickly around it, and dark swallowwort, and green maidenhair, and blooming parsley, and deergrass spreading through the marshy land. In the midst of the water the nymphs were arraying their games, the sleepless nymphs, dread goddesses of the country people, Eunice, and Malis, and Nycheia, with her April eyes. And now the boy was holding out the widemouthed pitcher to the water, intent on dipping it, but the nymphs all clung to his hand, sweetly restraining him, and they led him to a ferny knoll, where their steps crushed green smells into the dimming air. Then Amalmé, sacred to herself, lifted from its bed of hairy grass a disc of pink stone, with her blue hands of peace, and he heard faintly, like a half-remembered prophecy, the murmur of the soap spring. Dread Critasta bade him lie down, and she took him by the left foot, and Garga of the curled breasts by the right, and plunged him headmost naked into the plangent ooze, and as he sank into its benign suffocation even to his knees, he heard the tingling laughter and singing of the nymphs gathered about him in their holy circle, and the deaf padding of their feet in the itchy grass. When his brain had closed with morose darkness, and sorrow had filled his heart at the shame of life, they lifted him roughly out, and their laughter was an easy barking, and they cleaned the muddy suds from him with their spit and dried him with fronds of stinging nettles, writhing as he was, in the rigorous sheets soiled with his incontinence; dried and wiped him until he bled, and blood swelled his transparent gummy skin, and they licked and flailed him in turn, singing the rapid tangos of that land, and sucked and scratched his occasional bone, Garga whipping him with her leather dugs, Nanpreia stuffing his mouth with her acrid springy hair. And when the shame of death overtook him with a helpless spasm, and Nycheia's hands dripped his silver semen, came again Critasta with her shears to slit his seams and skin him deftly: and the bundle of his skin crackled in the fire that now flamed in the marsh, a fire of feathers, turds, and gray briers, while the nymphs in their frenzy shrieked small shrieks of nausea and hunger; and that smell was dear. Then the boy looked towards the setting sun, towards the companions he had lately left; and he saw his General, who had sent hot orders, and a galloper hurtled back for the horse which opened just as the last light fled up the hill to its summit and took refuge in the clouds; infantry appeared, and were pushed in among them and charged them, and, as night fell, they saw the breakup of the enemy, who abandoned all their stuff and went streaming up the col towards the two peaks of Mania, escaping into what they thought was empty land beyond. You

followed your mother into our orchard,
And with a disdain of years
I watched you pick wet apples.
My thirteenth year was on me
When that sight felled and terrible folly undid me.

5

Sever me from my appetent mind,
From the drum's glory, from the Dutch agio
Of dividends, bananas, and Christ's
Prayer, not from seduction not
From the limn of her limbs
nor the way of her waist
From the air of her hair   and the ease of her ears
From the bow of her elbow   and the shoal of her shoulders
From the tucks of her buttocks   and the wreath of her breath
From the hot of her heart   and the rain of her brain
From the soul of her soles   and the ash of her lashes
From the I of her eyes   and the fur of her forearm
From the bee of her bite   and the ouch of her touch
From the gum of her gums   and the pins of her nipples
From the musk of her muscles   and the trill of her nostrils
From the flan of her flanks   and the ice of her thighs
From the tug of her tongue in the south of her mouth
From the nave of her navel   and the fangs of her fingers
In the asp of her clasp, from the thump of her thumb
From the spines of her spine   and the rack of her back
From the leap of her lips   and the yank of her ankles
From the blur of her blood   and the bells of her breasts
From the lunge of her lungs   and the he of her hips
From the oh of her throat   and the uvula of her vulva
Yet the mouth of her belly are the heart of her feet
Yet the foot of her belly are the mouth of her heart

Yet the knees of her belly are the foot of her mouth
The hands of her eyes soft hurricanes
                                                            Seduction
    hrscht!
                                        sang
                                                            "garden
                                        The flowers speak in whispers (I
                                        Utter not a sound)
                                                                                                    snowing
                                        The flowers spoke in whispers and with
                                        Concern looked on: "Do not molest
                                        Our sister;
                                                            you sad and sallow man

Zum

Ha sawaram aoaf beaesarm

Zu zwurmu
Zehe essewearrmm eow bbeeeezz

Zehea
    zarozaarazinazg zasawazazm zaozof bzaezaezasz
                                                            bezz

                                                                            biz

Desire's everlasting
f
hairy s w
a
didn'd oil enema a
I'm sorry a
a
made him bend over drool
a a
"nates" rubberbelly
bluntfaced pubic shave a a
20 juicyfruit please footless
a
lined the Jews up I meant a
masterhole then I can't understand
drilled a
l Sieglinde!
sorry
l
ptlaarplop "wherever you are" "the machine a
of—— taste it?
a
know thyself a mass of bloody rubbish
will never junior
enis a
that time you
brown spots Mrs Pemberton lickle-lickle
a
kotex mirror "I love you"
with his truncheon would have a
sorry a
Tonto? a
no underpants?!
slim knife a
urp a
The smell r
m
golden

. . . .

Bells, mud, clouds, despair
My life was hers, now she is in it
There are sails, and blue summer, and impossibility
My bonebites soothe in a slush agglomeration
Mercury bubbles ascend: breath
My eyes cast a shadow of her outwards
My meaning confirms her absorbed altitude
The dog's gums yelp silence, silence
Her shadow pierces the dead serenities
The kayakist ignores the dull revelations
Sweet adoration of my dying existence
Little coils of her hair glitter
Verity's bitter nourishing honey
Supine in the pit or snow lake
Neither tressed anadems, nor baccar, nor amomum
"Goodbye, sweetheart, goodbye," she said, "Kenneth"
Immortal bees flit into the snow
Two wraiths face themselves, and lust
Orange snow suspends its collapse
What are you in the Delaware haze, X?
Rises between them in innocent devotion
In the doubled shadow you became I still
Her swimming shadow, the crash—sky!
Burn.

Comatas sang this as dusk came.

The Ring

Pierre put the gold in the morning into the ring-machine, and prayed. A sharp mallet swung anxiously in his hands, blades leapt from the agitation of his waiting feet; outside, trucks and cranes wheezed and clanged an aural incense into the tin-colored Paris sky. Paris! city of Jews and Antijews, of smitten children and child-coiffed flat eyes, where the meanness of the winter sun and the meanness of sausage-sellers beat as with their laden rubber chains the dark appetites of yearning—many reflections indited themselves on the casual slices of scrap copper that lay on the cement floor about the machine. The latter, also gray, was powered by twin anonymous engines; bakelite studs, whose double rectangular alignment banded the metal volumes with a uniform of final enclosure, vibrated blurringly sometimes, and when several hours' running had magnified the motor heat, emitted wasps of nostalgic smell. The mallet smashed aimlessly now the copper detritus, now the spread idle kneebones between which it shook. Some substance drifted from the. The telephone rang. "And what did it all mean? and what was it to be borne for? All those who are yet allowed the glory and honor of that glorious happiness, which comes from daring to order for the moment in their lives when they triumphantly love, 'the like for the like.'" Next it was time for lunch:

I began the pristine ascent. What if the flanks broke
Upon a depth of frozen honeys? The underskin of my forearms
Clutched upon shale. Gray thyme stood stiff in the small fissures,
Nameless blue spurts bloomed low; apples, lawns, and streams
Were known dryness drier than this wish. My body is there,
Not desire, not will: breathing, bruises—no beauty in the memory,
But hunger: holding a hot smoothed stone in my fist,
One with the spatial air towards the crest. In the dusky cwms
I await rainbow caverns, O forests of erect amber,
Cools of adept obsidian! After the approaches and before the last steepness
Was a tilted plane: there the stone roughness was muscled—
I looked back, far, lost, content, my calves twitched
From the painful irresistible push, I saw the ascent and its excitement;
Afterwards, less. Circular autumn
Will embrace the windy clambered peak. The precious ointment
In the flask of caves; and the light allows
A dun shadow under the egglike nacreous ridges. They did not come after me;
I returned through calm rainy woods. Some rocks as loose as milk teeth
Scrambled down and I clung to the grilled cliff with my tongue. Were there
        pools in the cooler heights
For the coming bliss of thirst? Hot boots suck upwards
From the boozy mud before a vast and intimate splendor
Where earth, stone, and shingle were nubile hatchings
In imperial day, with sweat in my mouth,
Sweetness in my lungs

        The pair return.
        There was no hope, yet through dissuasions of buttermetal
        Heaps, themselves, they join
        Where the olive-rank pales in resigned expectancy
        And of sun, in pools of silver dust
        Ascending easily high terrace to terrace

Over sheepflecked stiles, above the extended sea
Leaning on its russet stones
Where the wafted pines acknowledge redemption
Above pines
Sky, blue sombrero: the orange ground
Breaks with sweetwater and old rocks garlanded
The blue sky mounts?
The earth is fading orange
Swims cuprous instigation
There is too much to say
                                        fading bronze messengers
A sharp musics of loquat leaves
Observe their flight—both relief and ecstasy
O my love into the bronze bell
Steps, or sinking of a celestial tram
Some slight black foliage; fading earth; cliffs are of distant bronze
Let all the
The quick bright sea-blue
Pass, pass: Attend the sky,
    they're blue, passionate, invisible,
As your hand places the jar of blue crystals
By the waiting bath.

The Ledge

The dawn fog separated into two parts. The lower, a bluish translucent white, sank to earth in the shape of a lens, its edges resting against the bases of the mountains that defined the valley, its mass curving over the vague residue of the city. The upper part rose steadily, in silvery layers, like jellyfish gliding toward the surface of the ocean, in ever-increasing transparency. Into a cleft in the side of the valley a portion of the thinning fog was diverted from its ascent, was sucked into a bunched white river of cloud that flowed south, rising along the bed of the gorge that indented the mountain, to issue several miles farther on a high plateau. The cloud-river there flattened out over fields, enclosing the infrequent hamlets in moments of apparent bad weather, through which however the sun quickly penetrated, as the moisture continued its lateral dispersion. The valley-born cloud was no longer a cloud but an airy emulsion that tended toward the spruce forests on the hills edging the plateau, where it hung amid the dark trees long after the open areas had cleared. But other, truer clouds now appeared among and above the hills. For instance, to the south, puffs like explosions sailed into view; it is true that they did not last long. To the east where the higher hills lay, loglike clouds surged as the day warmed—they resembled the gorge cloud but were of a robuster nature, they did not cling in the forests but pushed over them, and even the hills did not alter the direction, only the inclination, of their advance. In the west, far away, flattish yellow-gray clouds drifted, looking as if they had lain between the pages of undusted tomes. Stared at, they were never seen to alter their position or shape. Yet after a glance to the north, where a tournament was about to start between contestants using cloud blocks, the western clouds had become unrecognizable: although still flat and immobile, they were in new parts of that section of the sky, and their outlines were no longer like chips but like blades. It was to those northern apparitions, however, that attention was directed during the noon and afternoon hours, not only because of the attractiveness of moving curves deployed on a grand scale, but because the spectacle was at once satisfyingly dramatic and satisfyingly remote. In fact those toppling towers seemed attached to the rim of a circle at whose center we, on the edge of the plateau, remained indefatigably vigilant: thus they rolled, flattening as they sank, slowly around from north to west and, at dusk, a little beyond. During their revolution they changed in color from cold-gray-tinged white through strawy yellow, in which the gray took on a darker tone, faint gold, rust and red to black, black at first streaked with sunset hues, then thick black. By this time the westerly flat clouds had risen high enough to refract daylight a while longer; and to the east the several logs of clouds had fused in one vast layer—it slides over the hilltops toward us like smoke from dry ice. The sky to the south is empty, and accompanied by the redness of the lofty western clouds, fluffed out now, this might lead us to expect a clear morning, but that anticipation is soon belied by the night sky, a sky of stars few and blurred.

Cassation on a Theme by Jacques Dupin

There is nothing left of the beat
In the proximate yielding of births
Down low, showered on, before May.
The slaves of the dreadful mind degrade you—
Start on your journey and enter the foothills.

Here the leaden falls will vanish
Achieving one tame agony
Out of a low mound of unopened ashes.
A vague repetition of the blessed cry will lift you up.
"Shall I lengthen my nights of pleasure? Shall I toss my useless emotions in the
air?"

There remains only the batter swirled
In the apogee of the fountain
On the rush-hour subway platform.
Ignoring the metrics beyond absolute silence, I preen my wings.
Shorten your worth. Bury your valuations.

The Dream-Work

for André du Bouchet

To this, speech already aspires—
Action its purpose and use
In forms incessantly renewed
To satisfy primal wishes:
The frame comes off the picture and strangles the viewer.
Words were dark implosions
Until pots that night
Of geraniums and wit
Tumbled from windows.
When speech is accorded to everyone,
Keep silence in the empty places
Where speech may be, undiscovered,
Unaccorded, issuing

Like yellow that bursts from a stream side,
illuminating
In the flash of its extinction.
(Let the air keep breathing this emptiness
Like a city emptied by night.)

The streets
Swarm with exact injunctions:
"What you know is not yours!"
We began modestly—he recounted
Techniques of exploitation,
You convince him that personality
Is not a class privilege.
Then while the crowd
Sang the old song
One taught the words
Fast against their numbers
(Canon by diminution)
And the foreign speaker
Dispensed with translation—
We cheered his sense
On Pentecost Monday
Dusty pigeons idle
A gift of lungs
Against the grift of tongues
"Fresh air at last!"
The agoraphobe in exaltation among thousands
The stammerer clear-tongued
The asthmatic jogs through the tear gas
Ex-students
Ex-professors
Ex-proles
With lids of red
In greenish night
Ex-"I"
Was that his name
Wasn't that his name
"Stella" zigzagging among grenades
Staying power against power
Some chucked back roachlike canisters as if matching airplanes
One bomber all thumbs but soccer-wise kicked thirty yards
the sizzling tube
A bleary bum tripped and got it, "accidental victim"

Reviving perception like black murder news
As they take to the streets:
"From the walls forth
To the world scene,
Dimmer cares to their ruck.
Whether forward
Whether freer,
Not for sinning and sinks.
My father's Mr. Nix,
In the foreign bins I climb,
Fine fare is not fine house,
My deck is not their dock.
With their fish glow
And their fruit stink
Let the finks die
In their stone slings.
Streaking in here
Flutes to the fun
With the wind
Over walled way
And the hymn—sick
Weepers, we're reapers to stay"

—at least, for a few days.

It was nothing like that.
Intimations piled on intimations—
Yellow burgeoning by a stream side
Wishes with similar shapes yet what
Means of evocation and exhaustion, a
Silence of saxophones upon tonic bees,
Suffering our oxygen sandwiches to sniff
The hushed liquid between smoke and smoke
Whose stream is unchanged, its waters everchanging,
Continuum licked by greenlipped nymphs with
Their noose of mongrels shining about us

"In a city garden, lofty acacias blooming by the gates,
A quince tree at the lawn's center, and at that end
rhododendrons
Pinked with shaggy blossom, she was unable
To explain how plan and councils
Might be reconciled.

In the first light, rust-colored stripes on her cheek
Changed from not-quite-credible to faint
Visibility in the brightening dusk"

Evening: I walk downhill along the Boulevard Raspail.
Purple seedless sunset rises over the city
Drenching everything in its bright slush.
Shop windows are shut and bluish. (It
That watches over the dream-work shall neither
Slumber nor snore.) I notice
An oil of still-smoking steamboats wrecked in the Seine;
A book, *The Philatelist Tong War*;
Illumination-brand cans of air from afar;
A nude made of grass or like stuff.
Words that will be redeemed by their abolition
Are meanwhile never pure abstraction;
But in times of latency, a necessary withdrawal—

Dusk,
Withdrawal,
"And this silence once again the light of day, falling
Around the silence sustained."
Above the stones and grass, light settles
Into blue gravel and shallows of orange dust,
Luminous ashes cascade over us
Without relief:

strenuous guys
War through the year
Towards other years.

Lateral Disregard

after an observation by Kenneth Koch

Shall I compare thee to a summer's bay
an orange cliff rising from its waters to the east
to the west a slope of reddish earth whorled with gray olives
between them an arc of rock, then sand, then little port
four houses of blue-washed rubble and red-tile roofs
and below them under broad-leaved vines a terrace with tables and benches
from which at noon the smoke of golden bream grilling
brings a gust of longing to the wayfarer as he looks over the bay
from a bluff down which a dusty zigzag path
leads to a straggly cluster of fig trees near the water's edge
(their first fruits now ripened in July sun)
to whose left on flat rocks ample nets have been drying
to whose right on the sand—green, yellow, green, red—four fishing craft
rest through the languid hours of the blue day
only at night taking to the clear dark waters
through which their bow-lights beckon curious fish
for nets to scoop from their nimble careers
to be shaken over the decks in slithering heaps
and at dawn the boats coast home between brighter blues
the glory of the world suffuses earth stone and leaf
land and sea reaffirm their distinction
in an exchange so gentle that the wayfarer briefly believes
he has been suspended lastingly in newborn light
the happiness and rightness of the morning
no longer dreaming plowing on through thick mud?

Ted Berrigan

Ted Berrigan was born in Providence, Rhode Island in 1934. He attended Providence College for a year before joining the army in 1954. Berrigan's stint in uniform lasted three years, and included an eighteen-month tour of duty in Korea. On his return to America in 1957 he enrolled in the University of Tulsa in Oklahoma, where he studied English and met the poets Ron Padgett and Dick Gallup, and the writer and artist Joe Brainard. In due course all four would gravitate to the Lower East Side of New York City, attracted both by the bohemian life-style and the prospect of meeting the poets and painters they most admired. In 1963 Berrigan founded *C: A Journal of Poetry*, which, in the mode of *Locus Solus*, published work by himself and his friends (the first issue was made up entirely of pieces by the Tulsa Four). The magazine soon attracted the attention of, and poems from, such as O'Hara, Koch, Schuyler and Ashbery, and the magazine developed into a forum for an intriguing dialogue between first- and second-generation New York poets – with a smattering of work by Beats thrown in for good measure, and with one issue featuring a cover by Andy Warhol.

Berrigan's *The Sonnets* (1964) make startling and inventive use of the techniques of collage and disjunction, splicing together lines from poems by such as Rimbaud, Apollinaire, Ashbery and O'Hara with snatches of overheard speech, snippets from newspapers and pulp fiction and letters, diary-like revelations, and never-explained references to times, places and names ('Dear Marge, hello. It is 5.15 a.m. / Andy Butt was drunk in the Parthenon'). Berrigan recycles these fragments over and over, like a resourceful street scavenger, and as the sequence expands it comes to resemble a vast labyrinth of echoes and allusions through which one stumbles and gropes, half-amused and half-baffled, searching for clues to the poems' shadowy, self-reflexive narrative. *The Sonnets* are both insistently literary, and seething with the grit and fumes and distractions of city life. The overarching narrative seems to involve an insoluble love triangle, but Berrigan's oblique methods allow him to conceal almost as much as he reveals. He was always interested in finding ways of opening his poetry to voices other than his own. He thrived in the collaborative atmosphere of the St Mark's Poetry Project, teaching workshops, giving readings, and organising events. His later work exhibits a directness that suggests the influence of the Beats, in particular Ginsberg; certainly poems such as 'Whitman in Black' and 'American Express' are less concerned than *The Sonnets* with technique. After years of ill health and amphetamine-use Berrigan died in 1983 at the age of forty-eight. His own epitaph, 'Last Poem', concludes: 'Let none regret my end who called me friend.'

from *The Sonnets*

I

His piercing pince-nez. Some dim frieze
Hands point to a dim frieze, in the dark night.
In the book of his music the corners have straightened
Which owe their presence to our sleeping hands.
The ox-blood from the hands which play
For fire for warmth for hands for growth
Is there room in the room that you room in?
Upon his structured tomb
Still they mean something. For the dance
And the architecture.
Weave among incidents
May be portentous to him
We are the sleeping fragments of his sky,
Wind giving presence to fragments.

XVII

for Carol Clifford

Each tree stands alone in stillness
After many years still nothing
The wind's wish is the tree's demand
The tree stands still
The wind walks up and down
Scanning the long selves of the shore
Her aimlessness is the pulse of the tree
It beats in tiny blots
Its patternless pattern of excitement
Letters   birds   beggars   books
There is no such thing as a breakdown
The tree   the ground   the wind   these are
Dear, be the tree your sleep awaits
Sensual, solid, still, swaying alone in the wind

XXIII

On the 15th day of November in the year of the motorcar
Between Oologah and Pawnee
A hand is writing these lines
In a roomful of smoky man names burnished dull black
Southwest, lost doubloons rest, no comforts drift
On dream smoke down the sooted fog ravine
In a terrible Ozark storm the Tundra vine
Blood ran like muddy inspiration: Walks he in around anyway
The slight film has gone to gray-green children
And seeming wide night. Now night
Is a big drink of waterbugs   Then were we so fragile
Honey scorched our lips
On the 15th day of November in the year of the motorcar
Between Oologah and Pawnee

XXX

Into the closed air of the slow
Now she guards her chalice in a temple of fear
Each tree stands alone in stillness
to gentle, pleasant strains
Dear Marge, hello. It is 5:15 a.m.
Andy Butt was drunk in the Parthenon
Harum-scarum haze on the Pollock streets
This excitement to be all of night, Henry!
Ah, Bernie, to think of you alone, suffering
It is such a good thing to be in love with you
On the green a white boy goes
He's braver than I, brother
Many things are current, and of these the least are
        not always children
On the 15th day of November in the year of the motorcar

XXXVI

after Frank O'Hara

It's 8:54 a.m. in Brooklyn it's the 28th of July and
it's probably 8:54 in Manhattan but I'm
in Brooklyn I'm eating English muffins and drinking
pepsi and I'm thinking of how Brooklyn is New
York city too how odd I usually think of it as
something all its own like Bellows Falls like Little
Chute like Uijongbu
                                        I never thought on the Williams-
burg bridge I'd come so much to Brooklyn
just to see lawyers and cops who don't even carry
guns taking my wife away and bringing her back
                                                                        No
and I never thought Dick would be back at Gude's
beard shaved off long hair cut and Carol reading
his books when we were playing cribbage and
watching the sun come up over the Navy Yard
across the river
                                    I think I was thinking when I was
ahead I'd be somewhere like Perry street erudite
dazzling slim and badly loved
contemplating my new book of poems
to be printed in simple type on old brown paper
feminine marvelous and tough

XXXVII

It is night. You are asleep. And beautiful tears
Have blossomed in my eyes. Guillaume Apollinaire is dead.
The big green day today is singing to itself
A vast orange library of dreams, dreams
Dressed in newspaper, wan as pale thighs
Making vast apple strides towards "The Poems."
"The Poems" is not a dream. It is night. You
Are asleep. Vast orange libraries of dreams
Stir inside "The Poems." On the dirt-covered ground
Crystal tears drench the ground. Vast orange dreams
Are unclenched. It is night. Songs have blossomed
In the pale crystal library of tears. You
Are asleep. A lovely light is singing to itself,
In "The Poems," in my eyes, in the line, "Guillaume
    Apollinaire is dead."

LV

"Grace to be born and live as variously as possible"
Frank O'Hara

Grace to be born and live as variously as possible
White boats   green banks   black dust   atremble
Massive as Anne's thighs upon the page
I rage in a blue shirt at a brown desk in a
Bright room sustained by a bellyful of pills
"The Poems" is not a dream   for all things come to them
Gratuitously   In quick New York we imagine the blue Charles
Patsy awakens in heat and ready to squabble
No Poems she demands in a blanket command   belly
To hot belly we have laid   serenely white
Only my sweating pores are true in the empty night
Baffling combustions are everywhere!   we hunger and taste
And go to the movies   then run home drenched in flame
To the grace of the make-believe bed

LIX

In Joe Brainard's collage its white arrow
does not point to William Carlos Williams.
He is not in it, the hungry dead doctor.
What is in it is sixteen ripped pictures
Of Marilyn Monroe, her white teeth white-
washed by Joe's throbbing hands. "Today
I am truly horribly upset because Marilyn
Monroe died, so I went to a matinee B-movie
and ate King Korn popcorn," he wrote in his
Diary. The black heart beside the fifteen pieces
of glass in Joe Brainard's collage
takes the eye away from the gray words,
Doctor, but they say "I LOVE YOU"
and the sonnet is not dead.

LXXIV

"The academy of the future is opening its doors"
John Ashbery

The academy of the future is opening its doors
my dream a crumpled horn
Under the blue sky the big earth is floating into "The Poems."
"A fruitful vista, this, our South," laughs Andrew to his Pa.
But his rough woe slithers o'er the land.
Ford Madox Ford is not a dream. The farm
was the family farm. On the real farm
I understood "The Poems."
Red-faced and romping in the wind, I, too,
am reading the technical journals. The only travelled sea
that I still dream of
is a cold black pond, where once
on a fragrant evening fraught with sadness
I launched a boat frail as a butterfly

LXXVI

I wake up back aching from soft bed Pat
gone to work Ron to class (I
never heard a sound) it's my birthday. I put on
birthday pants birthday shirt go to ADAM's buy a
pepsi for breakfast come home drink it take a pill
I'm high. I do three Greek lessons
to make up for cutting class. I read birthday book
(from Joe) on Juan Gris real name José Vittoriano
Gonzáles stop in the middle read all
my poems gloat a little over new ballad quickly skip old
sonnets imitations of Shakespeare. Back to books. I read
poems by Auden Spenser Pound Stevens and Frank O'Hara.
    I hate books.
            I wonder if Jan or Helen or Babe
ever think about me. I wonder if Dave Bearden still
dislikes me. I wonder if people talk about me
secretly. I wonder if I'm too old. I wonder if I'm fooling
myself about pills. I wonder what's in the icebox. I wonder
if Ron or Pat bought any toilet paper this morning

Words for Love

for Sandy

Winter crisp and the brittleness of snow
as like make me tired as not. I go my
myriad ways blundering, bombastic, dragged
by a self that can never be still, pushed
by my surging blood, my reasoning mind.

I am in love with poetry. Every way I turn
this, my weakness, smites me. A glass
of chocolate milk, head of lettuce, dark-
ness of clouds at one o'clock obsess me.
I weep for all of these or laugh.

By day I sleep, an obscurantist, lost
in dreams of lists, compiled by my self
for reassurance. Jackson Pollock   René
Rilke   Benedict Arnold   I watch
my psyche, smile, dream wet dreams, and sigh.

At night, awake, high on poems, or pills
or simple awe that loveliness exists, my lists
flow differently. Of words bright red
and black, and blue.   Bosky.   Oubliette.   Dis-
severed. And O, alas

Time disturbs me. Always minute detail
fills me up. It is 12:10 in New York. In Houston
it is 2 p.m. It is time to steal books. It's
time to go mad. It is the day of the apocalypse
the year of parrot fever! What am I saying?
Only this. My poems do contain
wilde beestes. I write for my Lady
of the Lake. My god is immense, and lonely
but uncowed. I trust my sanity, and I am proud. If
I sometimes grow weary, and seem still, nevertheless

my heart still loves, will break.

Personal Poem #7

for John Stanton

It is 7:53 Friday morning in the Universe
New York City to be somewhat exact
I'm in my room wife gone working Gallup
fucking in the room below

                        had 17½ milligrams desoxyn
last night 1 Miltown, read Paterson, parts
1 & 2, poems by Wallace Stevens & How Much Longer
Shall I Be Able To Inhabit The Divine Sepulchre
(John Ashbery). Made lists of lines to
steal, words to look up (didn't). Had steak & eggs
with Dick while Sandy sweetly slept.

At 6:30 woke Sandy
fucked til 7 now she's late to work & I'm still
high. Guess I'll write to Bernie today
and Tom. And call Tony. And go out at 9 (with Dick)
to steal books to sell, so we can go
to see A NIGHT AT THE OPERA

Personal Poem #8

It's 5:03 a.m. on the 11th of July this morning
and the day is bright gray turning green   I can't stop
loving you says Ray Charles   and I know exactly
what he means because the Swedish policeman in the
next room is beating on my door demanding sleep
and not Ray Charles and bluegrass   does he know
that in three hours I go to court to see if the world
will let me have a wife   he doesn't of course it wouldn't
occur to him   nor would it occur to him to write
"scotch-tape body" in a notebook but it did occur to
John Stanton alias The Knife Fighter age 18 so why
are my hands shaking I should know better

Living with Chris

for Christina Gallup

It's not exciting to have a bar of soap
in your right breast pocket
it's not boring either
it's just what's happening in America, in 1965

If there is no Peace in the world
it's because there is no Peace
in the minds of men. You'd be surprised, however
at how much difference
a really good cup of coffee & a few pills can make
in your day

I would like to get hold of
the owner's manual
for a 1965 model "DREAM"
(Catalogue number CA-77)

I am far from the unluckiest woman in the world

I am far from a woman

An elephant is tramping in my heart

Alka-Seltzer Palmolive Pepsodent Fab
Chemical New York

There is nothing worse than elephant love

Still, there is some Peace in the world. It is
night. You are asleep. So I must be at peace

The barometer at 29.58 and wandering

But who are you?

For god's sake, is there anyone out there listening?

If so, Peace.

American Express

Cold rosy dawn in New York City
not for me
in Ron's furlined Jim Bridger
(coat)
that I borrowed two years ago
had cleaned
but never returned, Thank god!
On 6th Street
Lunch poems burn
a hole is in my pocket
two donuts one paper bag
in hand
hair is in my face and in my head is
"cold rosy dawn in New York City"
I woke up this morning
it was night
you were on my mind
on the radio
And also there was a letter
and it's to you
if "you" is Ron Padgett,
American express
shivering now in Paris
Oklahoma
two years before
buying a new coat for the long trip
back to New York City
that I'm wearing now

It is cold in here
for two
looking for the boll weevil
(looking for a home), one with pimples
one blonde, from Berkeley
who says, "Help!" and
"Hey, does Bobby Dylan come around here?"
"No, man," I say,
"Too cold!"
& they walk off, trembling,
(as I do in L.A.)

so many tough guys, faggots, & dope addicts!
though I assure them
"Nothing like that in New York City!"
It's all in California!
(the state state)
that shouldn't be confused with
The balloon state
that I'm in now
hovering over the radio
following the breakfast of champions
& picking my curious way
from left to right
across my own white
expansiveness
MANHATTAN!
listen
The mist of May
is on the gloaming
& all the clouds
are halted, still
fleecy
& filled
with holes.
They are alight with borrowed warmth,
just like me.

"I Remember"

I remember painting "I HATE TED BERRIGAN" in big black letters
    all over my white wall.
I remember bright orange light coming into rooms in the late afternoon.
    Horizontally.
I remember when I lived in Boston reading all of Dostoyevsky's
    novels one right after the other.
I remember the way a baby's hand has of folding itself around
    your finger, as tho forever.
I remember a giant gold man, taller than most buildings, at
    "The Tulsa Oil Show."
I remember in Boston a portrait of Isabella Gardner by Whistler.
I remember wood carvings of funny doctors.
I remember opening jars that nobody else could open.
I remember wondering why anyone would want to be a doctor. And
    I still do.
I remember Christmas card wastebaskets.
I remember not understanding why Cinderella didn't just pack up and
    leave, if things were all *that* bad. I remember "Korea."
I remember one brick wall and three white walls.
I remember one very hot summer day I put ice cubes in my aquarium
    and all the fish died.
I remember how heavy the cornbread was. And it still is.

Joseph Ceravolo

Joseph Ceravolo was born in the Astoria district of Queens in 1934. He was the son of first generation Italian immigrants, both of whom worked in the garment industry: his father was a custom tailor for Saks Fifth Avenue, and his mother a seamstress. Ceravolo began writing poetry in his early twenties, while stationed in Germany during a tour of service in the US Army. In 1959 he enrolled in Kenneth Koch's now legendary Poetry Workshop at the New School for Social Research. Over the next few years he met many of the writers associated with the New York School. He became particularly close to Ted Berrigan, but never embraced, as Berrigan did, the bohemian lifestyle of the Lower East Side counter-culture. Rather, like his great hero William Carlos Williams, Ceravolo sought to balance his creative life with the business of earning a living and the responsibilities of raising a family. He trained and worked as a civil engineer, specialising in hydraulics, and settled with his wife and three children in Bloomfield, New Jersey. His first collection, *Fits of Dawn*, was published by Berrigan's C Press in 1965, and this was followed by *Spring in This World of Poor Mutts*, winner of the 1968 Frank O'Hara Book Award, *Transmigration Solo* in 1979, and *Millennium Dust* in 1982. A volume of Ceravolo's selected poetry, *The Green Lake is Awake*, appeared in 1994, six years after his sudden death from cancer of the bile duct.

Kenneth Koch has praised the 'amazing perceptual archaeology' of Ceravolo's poetry, and in a review of *Transmigration Solo* Peter Schjeldahl declared: 'Ceravolo is a lyric poet of such oddness and purity that reading him all but makes me feel dizzy, like exercise at a very high altitude.' Ceravolo shares with James Schuyler the ability to infuse simple declarative statements with a peculiar poignancy and vulnerability, allowing us to feel the ordinariness and uniqueness of a particular moment or observation. His work, again like Schuyler's, makes inventive use of the traditions of pastoral; Ceravolo's poems habitually refer to the weather, the seasons, clouds, birds, the sea, fish and animals, though his use of ellipses and semi-surreal imagery works to overlay his landscapes with a delicate haze, as if one were viewing them through a fragile, trembling veil. At his best his work seems both intimate and curiously recessed, his descriptions at once vivid, tentative, and oblique. Ceravolo may lack the energy and brashness of poets such as O'Hara and Berrigan, but his subtle reworkings of the conventions of nature poetry often result in an almost trance-like awareness of the rhythms of time and nature, and the patterns created by our forms of attention.

Caught in the Swamp

High is the dark clouds
and the harbor and
the egg as the antelope
frightens us through the
swampy harbor. We burn
our food, and the egg
has a seal of abandon
                    in its blueness.
Which are we humming at last?
It is the running of the shiny antelope
we smell, not love.
Is it the bed?

After the Rain

The soap is wet from the storm
and then it is lost
. . . .
I am peeking out.
I feel a chill across
the forehead
The breeze. The toy gun . . .
The quiet birds,
not as quiet as the cork

from this bottle we
drank last night

Dusk

Before the dusk grows deeper
Now comes a little moth dressed in
rose pink, wings bordered with yellow. Now
a tiger moth, now another and another   another

Heart Feels the Water

The fish are staying here
and eating. The plant is
thin and has very long leaves
like insects' legs, the way
they bend down.
Through the water
the plant breaks from the water:

the line of the water and the air.
Told!

Lighthouse

All this summer fun.
The big waves, and waiting
(the moon is broken)
for the moon to come out
and revive the water. You look
and you want to watch as
men feel the beer breaking
on their lips, and women seem like
the sun on your little back.
Where are you closer to everything?
in the plants? on the photograph or
the little heart that's not
used to beating like the waves' foam?
            A wasp is
looking for a hole in the screen.
No. There's no man in the lighthouse.
There's no woman there, but there is
a light there; it is a bulb.
And I think how complete you are
in its light. Flash . . . . Flash . . . . .
. . . .
And I think of how our room
will smell; You lying on one bed
and we in the other,
facing the . . . flash . . . . .
. . . . Flash

The Wind is Blowing West

1

I am trying to decide to go swimming,
But the sea looks so calm.
All the other boys have gone in.
I can't decide what to do.

I've been waiting in my tent
Expecting to go in.
Have you forgotten to come down?
Can I escape going in?
I was just coming

I was just going in
But lost my pail

2

A boisterous tide is coming up;
I was just looking at it.
The pail is near me
again. My shoulders have sand on them.

Round the edge of the tide
Is the shore. The shore
Is filled with waves.
They are tin waves.

Boisterous tide coming up.
The tide is getting less.

3

Daytime is not a brain,
Living is not a cricket's song.
Why does light diffuse
As earth turns away from the sun?

I want to give my food
To a stranger. I want
to be taken.
What kind of a face do

I have while leaving?
I'm thinking of my friend.

4

I am trying to go swimming
But the sea looks so calm
All boys are gone
I can't decide what to do

I've been waiting to go
Have you come down?
Can I escape

I am just coming
            Just going in

May

I am lost.
I had swum before.
There is no deformation fatigue
Residual under salt water
Morning oh May flower! oh
May exist. Built.
When will water stop
cooling? Built, falling. Reeds. I am surprised.
Weakness. Torsion.
The wind, white.
Sapphire, oxidation. Million . . . . . .

Warmth

There's nothing to love in this
rice Spring.
Collected something warm like friends.
Sail glooms are none.
Your desire
rests like sailors in
their bunks. Have beaten you, lips.
Supply me
man made keeping.
Supply it flowing out;
are brute bullets in your back
because there is
in this rice Spring

White Fish in Reeds

Hold me
till only,   these are my
        clothes   I sit.
Give them   more songs than
the flower
These are my clothes to a
boat   Streets
have no feeling
Clouds move

Are people woman?
Who calls you
on a sun shirt sleeves down his ecstasy
The hair you are
becoming? Mmmm

That this temperate is where
I feed   The sheep sorrel flower is
And I want to
be
among all things
that bloom
Although I do not
love flowers

Indian Suffering

Look, ah, dry
streets, still
not a gorged begin, he time in
you love,
cruel. What are
we doing to our faces? He waits
to grow up. Who
are you when you don't grow? Would it
mean to usually
range animal things that
satisfy? Is nature a day begun?
Bow wow wow I am
going home.
The children called
him ugly boy. I am not
afraid of
anything. Boy-not-afraid.
Ugly boy a magic.

Sculpture

The dogs are barking.
I am cutting.
Am cutting like the
sounds of the sniffling
baby in the momma's
        womb. The sniffle is clean.
Now the night isn't black.
How is night not over,
cuddling us from the dark?
                (It's over)
Day has cut.
Now I have to get something.
The sun has cut
            into the dirty glass.

Pregnant, I Come

I come to you
with the semen
and the babies:
ropes of the born.

I rise up as you go up
in your consciousness.
Are you unhappy
in the source?

The clouds sputter
across the ring.
Do the birds sing?

Is the baby singing in you?   yet.

Spring in this World of Poor Mutts

I kiss your lips
on a grain: the forest,

the fifth, how many do
you want on here?
This is the same you
I kiss, you hear
me, you help:

I'm thirty years old.
I want to think in summer now.
Here it goes, here it's summer

(A disintegrated robot)
over us.
We are mortal. We ride
the merry-go-round. A drummer like
this is together.
Let's go feel the water.
              Here it goes!

Again and it's morning "boom"
                      autumn
"boom" autumn
and the corn is sleeping.
It is sleeping and sweating
and draws the beautiful
soft green sky.

Walk home with the
animal on my shoulder
in the river, the river gets
deeper   , the Esso gets
deeper; morning,
          morning,
          cigarette,
family and animal
and parents along the river.
Oh imagination. That's how I need you.

A flying duck or an antler refrains.
The small deer at the
animal farm walks up
to us.

A waterbug comes into
the bathroom.
The north sky is all frozen over
like a river.
Like a pimple a waterbug
comes into us
and our lives are full
of rivers. Heavy waterbug!

This is the robot and he
continues across the street.
Looking at a bird
his penis is hanging down;
a wind for
its emotions.
    I don't want to sleep.
The cold around my arms.
Like an iron lung.
As sleep comes closer to the robot's
emotion. Iron.

Spring. Spring. Spring. . . . . .
            Spring!
Spring down! come down!
There it goes! there it goes!
Arm belly strike.
Press friend push.
Teeth cruel arrow. I cannot
do without,
without do I cannot, Spring.

Chrome gladly press.
Between me, my wings. Listen as
the fireflies organize.
O save me, this Spring, please!
Before I hurt her
        I hurt her only life
        too much
and it carries in this
iron bug crawling all around.
            Is this Spring?
and it carries me,
iron bug, through the Spring.

A Song of Autumn

A dog disappears
across a small lake.
It waits for me.
It goes where I want to go.
Begins to wake up the flowers.
So leave us alone.
Because no freedom can choose
between faces and
hours as destroyed as moving,
or cold water in the
sun. I can go out
now and measure
the flies that swing around trees
like doctors around a woman
full of bars and beauties
you could never make free;
Not even if the
flowers turn to moss and
loose sensations for their stems.

I Like to Collapse

  Saturday night   I buy a soda
Someone's hand opens   I hold it
It begins to rain
Avenue A   is near the river

Autumn-Time, Wind and the Planet Pluto

Like a spear afterwards
cut out,
head and eye hurts "When is he
coming to wear me because I
am a prisoner
full of victims
and human" she said

He was the only one with
a skin disease.
Tied to, he fell "I love him" She fell
like a stone on a rope
and instead death instead of arms free

Sun testicles next
of splashes

Drunken Winter

Oak oak! like like
it then
cold some wild paddle
so sky then;
flea you say
"geese geese" the boy
June of winter
of again
Oak sky

Wild Provoke of the Endurance Sky

Be uncovered!
Hoe with look life!   Sun rises.
Rice of suffering. Dawn
          in mud,
this is roof   my friend
O country   o cotton   drag
of the wild provoke,
there's a thousand years   How are
you growing?
No better to in a stranger.
Shack, village,
                    brother,
wild provoke of the endurance sky!

Grow

I fight and fight.
I wake up.
The oasis is now dark.
I cannot hear anything.

The wind is felt
and the stars and the sand
so that no one
will be taken by pain.

I sit next to the bushes,
Hercules couldn't move me,
and sleep and dream.

The sand, the stars are solid
in this sleeping oasis,
alone with the desert and
the metaphysical cigarette.

Dangers of the Journey to the Happy Land

Talk of energy.   Mayan sub-flower
Come to light and feel physically intent to
plasm
      Even if I don't share
      Instance the mother
Talk of energy or stolen from her
mother
          I didn't do that for
nothing   I speak as a wife to the
capsizing   Both are once
Perspire like an autumn wind bakes. Mayan
sub-flowers.
      Am I allowed to go to
the tough section?   That's tough.
         Mayan sub-flowers in
             the shade.

Bill Berkson

Bill Berkson was born in New York in 1939. He grew up on the Upper East Side, just off the Museum Mile. He attended Trinity School and then Brown University, but abandoned his studies there in his second year and returned to Manhattan after reading an issue of *The Evergreen Review* that contained poems by Allen Ginsberg, Gregory Corso, and Frank O'Hara. Something was happening, he realised, and he wanted to find out what it was. Berkson quickly developed into a pivotal figure in the New York 60s art and poetry scenes. He studied with Koch at the New School, and then ran poetry workshops there himself, where his pupils included Bernadette Mayer and Patti Smith; he collaborated with O'Hara on a series of poems called *Hymns of St. Bridget* (1961–4); he wrote articles and reviews for *Art News*, freelanced for the Museum of Modern Art, and had his first volume, *Saturday Night: Poems 1960-61*, issued by John Bernard Myers for Tibor de Nagy Editions, who also published the first volumes of Ashbery, Koch, and O'Hara. Its title is borrowed from a painting by Willem de Kooning, and Berkson has written extensively on artists such as de Kooning, Jackson Pollock, Franz Kline, Hans Hofmann, Jasper Johns, and Philip Guston, who provided drawings for Berkson's 1975 collection, *Enigma Variations*. A selection of his art criticism has been published in the volume *The Sweet Singer of Modernism and Other Art Writings* (2004).

In 1970 Berkson moved to Bolinas in Northern California, where a number of poets associated with the St Mark's Poetry Project, including Lewis Warsh, Joanne Kyger, and Tom Clark had recently settled, establishing what was in effect a chapter of the New York School in this small rural town an hour's drive north of San Francisco. There Berkson started up his own small press called Big Sky, which published a poetry journal, poetry books, and *Homage to Frank O'Hara* (1978). Since 1993 he has lived in San Francisco, where he teaches. In recent years he has curated exhibitions by such as George Herriman, Ronald Bladen, and George Schneeman. If Berkson's poetic roots are undoubtedly in the New York of the 1960s, his work also makes use of – and has been influential on – certain developments in West Coast avant-garde poetics. He has a gift for outrageous similes ('pools of smoke that smell ridiculously like someone's raised eyebrow in a cyclone') and for kaleidoscopic refractions of the language and textures that surround us. As Ron Padgett has observed, Berkson's multifaceted, openended compositions are 'shot through with a gorgeous abstraction', and shimmer on the page like a web of 'brilliant hookups between eye, ear, mind, and heart'.

October

I

It's odd to have a separate month. It
escapes the year, it is not only cold, it is warm
and loving like a death grip on a willing knee. The
Indians have a name for it, they call it:
"Summer!" The tepees shake in the blast like roosters
at dawn. Everything is special to them,
the colorful ones.

II

Somehow the housewife does not seem gentle.
Is she angry because her husband likes October?
Is it snow bleeds softly from her shoes?
The nest eggs have captured her,
but April rises from her bed.

III

"The beggars are upon us!" cried Chester.

Three strangers appeared at the door, demanding ribbons.

The October wind . . . nests

IV

Why do I think October is beautiful?
It is not, is not beautiful.
                                        But then
what is there to hold one's interest
between the various driftings of a day's
work, but to search out the differences . . .
                              the window and grate—
but it is not, is not
beautiful.

V

I think your face is beautiful, the way it is
close to my face, and I think you are the real
October with your transparence and the stone
of your words as they pass, as I do not hear them.

All You Want

The alarm of a lighter morning breathes before your eyes
in pools of smoke that smell ridiculously like someone's raised eyebrow in a
cyclone.
It is complete to be dying, slightly, today, and to want as if the leaf
of your thoughts were pointing upwards at a field of hay in which a savage
has stuck some awful message: "The soap is in your eyes, the fever's at your
feet,
where you sit is a honeycomb on which you're stuck and it's safe to avoid the
pleasures
of the threshold." Sunday is like any other day of wires
stretched across your torso like a tie of red and gold on which a clock has set
its chimes. it's dull to always weave a serpent from the air, and all the levees
have sunk beneath your boat that goes and never falters like the clock striking
two
(the bars have opened, the churches have closed), and everything will have
a gleaming ring of stones around it as the windows remain full of palms.
To "open": a precarious waking, the wrists turned upwards. And you know
that sentimentality is the razor you walk on as a bird finds its boring nest.
Sparks are strewn about the sidewalk, August is a matchbook, and your hearts
flit with violence for striking in the surf of what you hope is activity
with your chest bared to the closing room of what you are and all you want.

Breath

November! November! Smoke outrunning branches, reefs
turning hideous and cold, windows accepting porches
accepting the draft, the dust, its vacancies like the arctic
desert . . . the lead-dogs in heat, thirst of adventurers
for elastic, the bench, walk, and fountain certainties!
It is definitely a city like the top of something, the pole!

So we went walking in our breath—denying the tooth of it,
It was the sandwich, drying quickly color-deletion propellers
The conditioned button on our ears, we fastened it, shinily
being smart—November will not outlast it, it is a straight
red line around the heart's jacket, forming a gray one, it is
fur, fur for steel as ourselves, run it on your fingertip grate
like picking up a pencil, aware of the next-door cellar of fire
Mush! pull from out under the cellophane considered knocking, was it
candy, glue, a stick of bells? Snows snow on the mountain pedals—
it has not arrived immediately "they will be late as scissors"
"they will be early as the knob"

The drawer finished and the collection without doubt burned
at its edges, beginning a new crossing with real paint, lacking
as would have it hinge a real armies with which to deal
Love comes but once to a shoe
and must be stepped on
if we, any of us, are to
survive . . . in its tracks, the moth
capered like his sailor-suit photo against,
my speedy dessert season, an armistice wrested from the trees

Russian New Year

for Norman Bluhm

Now trouble comes between the forest's selves,
And smoke spreads to pools in which we stroke
Our several smirks, but the accident will not happen
For someone has stolen the apples
And someone else has "come full circle", picked at the fog.
Snow settled in the meetinghouse. "I love you as my own dear jailbird.
I cannot think of you without thinking of the New York lighting system."
Shame sneaks in the birches, a fire has been put out.
The distance is too much again, an army is raising the dust—
Are these horses we count as pets?

It is whiter than your face the afternoon I opened your icebox.
You are entitled to it, wisdom which bores us but may excite you
By the glint the pillows made on the horizon, unwounding silences
Mixing the poison I breathe and leave behind me
At the hitching post
                                        Her dress raised above her ears
She lay livid among the party favors   She closed her
Umbrella   It is a cape of black which turned the carousel
It is a bucket into which night has fallen   It is no fun
Light and happy, the canyon.

My days are eaten slowly.
The pricks incorporate all jolly in the lurch.
I sit on the fluorescent seat.
All revolutions have betrayed themselves
By slush of feeling
For the rose will shoot from the ground
As buildings stick in the wind and stop it a minute
Someone will remain
Of life riding into the trees to grow up
A steamy stormer of storms.

Are you different from that shelter you
Built for knives? On the sidewalk, sapphires.
On the fifth floor, fungus was relaxing. I have put on
The crimson face of awakeness you gave me
What is that heart-shaped object that thaws your fingers?
It is a glove and in it a fist.

The shore slides out of the sea
To live privately beneath the noise
Of the sandbar budging
A rose above the eagle   it was there
Tattooed   Sumac above us   Pain
Is spliced and ticked away by waiting
In the chair beneath which paste is dripping
And a match is lit
From today on it is sleep I leave you on the slow waterfall
One cannot even escape light
On the night's horizon, you believe that is pleasant,
Don't you?   Or when it is snowing heat remains
In the cupboard—that too? . . . Thunder?
With you it is always the inconspicuous tear
With me it is never anything but money
Still we are the same . . . Sideways

Strawberry Blond

Knock on the forehead
there, there beach nothings
saw, reef, watery exchanges
of lift O's not followed by
anything turf   True?
(ringlet) (broadcast)
in wing around immortal portraits, are they?
the be-hanged cunieform
money sniff)

rung-ticker
a refusing passion
for burn on, brief nail!
under the sheets a lip
hits the sulfur stripe
phone book being a strength
(a) (its Irish sequel)
(b) paralysis   mustard
back on the office
the rifting phlox
looks and wins
what cabinet of ruse and doubt
give him the possibility of love and
honor though her eyes, a doubtful sign of rain showing up on
the backporch on which they swang out the years of his death
and on which she sat like an expectant mother—that was unblackened!

Chocolate
tiding over the gray embittered court

he prayed for his marriage
as was the modern custom   as if promiscuity were
well, Stupid!   finding tics

What am I inditing that heads off   gardenia?

green green stovepipe

arm around me stalk wherein pegged a relax bus
globule of often-candelabra in the cake
of soap she saw her face a few times
feather in his blood
margin   eat shit if
in it old waterhole
rub-down, shower, and melted

in her sleep

he woke up

they went off   socks

Variation

Half-ended melodies are purer.
To no longer perform in broad daylight,
the apple's a radish for it,
the winter chill a living thing.
But take your brother in later learning:
Let the girls who will smell the buried cloves there.

So I am only beginning to learn what I from time to time forget.
But throw away these childish things!

Barney's coffin disappeared,
and luckily you said the right thing
for the sky mentioned for the last time.
The little master of smalltalk
is really the seducer of your every move,
taking you into his confidence the way a cat his mouse.

And still young Lycidas cannot express himself fully.
(And) "Everyone is the same"

even down to his jockey shorts, *dolce far niente*, as they say.

Out There

for Jasper Johns

Rain and the thought of rain:
but reality won't make itself over for the fact that you sense something—
won't in fact wax miraculous,
though it's right—that responsibility belongs to the outer ether whose
fragments are gummed together
so as to be analyzable only *in toto*. So
the man who cries "Marvelous!" is only human, putting out his sign. But
the ether doesn't need this sign.
Cloudburst to terrace to drainpipe backalley sewage to river to sea—
No need, my love, to complain.
Quieting down.
Going on inside.

Booster

You go down to go up.
In theory, this is fine.
But the odds are the plane falling through the sky at what
miraculous rate!
will never see that sky again—it flaps to ground.
What ensues is too horrible to relate.
But suppose
you stopped the picture at just that instant—
two miles up!
The silver bird caught in delicate half-turn.
something like a swan dive with a twist.
You can't see, no matter how you magnify it,

the faces of the passengers
in flight;
close as you can get, they're just a series of blurs,
slightly "off" details within
this beautiful sight.

Blue Is the Hero

leading with his chin, though bristling
with military honor, camp and *ora pro nobis,* rolling out
the red carpet of chance on a plea
that you might give others a front-row seat:
Lady, take off your hat. So extra special . . .
Other times, it would be a roof garden
like the one Rauschenberg has,
being no Nebuchadnezzar of the bush,
or, standing on your head,
feeling the earth has "hung" a lawn
and these dogs have come to bite you "where it hurts"—
I wonder if they've really caught the scent,
which is a poor memory on our Symbolist ears
of what it must have been like to read *The Hound*
of the Baskervilles for the first time in 1899
oh truly modern and amused and wrong,
before the world, before the cold
and the dry vermouth and everybody started
wearing sweaters, taking pills. I confess
to a certain yearning in my genes for those trips,
tonics of the drawn shade and rumpled bed,
the Albergo delle Palme in Palermo, instead
of hanging on the curb, learning to love each
latest gem "fantastic!" as the lights go out all over the
Flatiron Building, which leaves the moon, sufficiently
fa so la, and the clouds
disentangle a perfect Mondrian, pure gray,
to which you give nodding assent, somewhat true—
you are that helicopter, primping for the climb
into whose bed of historical certainty? the fuel
streaming down the sides, like fun in the sun, air in the air.

Roots

The people round off this planet

in spheres of sharp perfection

prickly, blithe

as the jawbone

of a spiritualist's peevish

ups and downs.

However, these bubbles

could care less,

stuck, I guess,

in familiar gnawing sleep

between the lights

of droning planes

as the people undress

persuasive and abundant

inside the lens

its knowing glance

forever equals

the amazing ability to forget

Fourth Street, San Rafael

There was an old man at the bank today
Standing beside the paying/receiving window while his wife
Cashed a check or made a deposit she wore a light
Blue dress black shoes black hair
Not a sign of white or gray in it
But from the curve her shoulders made a weight sunk
Down to her ankles she was probably of a certain age
Though a few years younger than her husband
Whose ripened aging was no way disguised
A stiff olive drab fishing cap visor above his long bony face
And around his neck he had on one of those thong ties old gents wear
With a metal clasp at the collar and blunt tips at the ends
Loose hung sports jacket and baggy no-color slacks with a belt
He stood talking seriously to her about their money matters
And whenever he wanted to make some special point
He would place his hand firmly on her back and pat or caress it
With such decorum he would be her constant lover any time
Healthy wealthy and wise, and so it seemed
Stepping up to the adjoining window next in line

A Fixture

Not ever knowing what she does in the shower,
a frictional sorrow like bedding in dark
feeling brows flex over wireless concerns,
not hers.
A stone in the river you can't move moves you.
And the postholes wobble. Glaze is permanent.

In her partition is the stairway of unhunched love,
a muscular mouth.

Instinct

A mildly hostile point
breaks across the table
and is an organ of breathing
much as Hector and / or Ajax enthusing
over the Oxford Origins of Cures.

She always gets the dish the others can just about stand.
Then I'm sick to my stomach, writing off morsels the oven's already
turned down. Ever a tale of brooding capillaries
exposing a genre of matched sets: isocolor sweatshirt and grandma's
earrings, a fuzzy muffler and muff.

The table gets rounder than was guessed.
Its imagery's dowels are trained to bid us
become the masters of our age, not to act it.
No suspicious empathy, ambassadorial
to make solvable the hornet's trick of dream
as childhood's taller girls' in closets meant.
And if a tree falls to the ground
the earth will close and crown it.

A Head at the Covers

I removed the rains and motored
and flipped through the covers of a board
a card with shavings labeled to a lace cross
in the mirror-narrow confines of an
eyesore fog you can fly
over still and put
your finger on a dune

as if pins were
to be pushed dimly
inches downward from
a manila star

What if the panic is on
and this parrot weather
has crows feet
which aren't a regular part of the job
but the deep end of a lot of things
that leak their loads like twigs to the vortex
an uphill travail

Unlivable sounds stem from the woodworks
traipse on the back of an igneous broom
that busses bees to certain rarity

but I'm with
the sun bolting
all the ledges
my odd blue dots anchored
I barely think to what
since what has gone and merged

The whole inch piles on gathered corks
the strips in place are a snore of blue
a while so lifted you watch it shatter care,
lacking evidence, with personnel to spare
I left a face spinning on the stair

In a Hand Not My Own

A blank wall is singing
to be separate from the rest.
It is too mild for the casually attired
to be living among their glittery glassine poses.
Or else my superstitions are wrong,
built sideways from a limb, or anyhow panting.

But why fuss? If personality were legal tender,
ours would pass for coin of the realm. As
it is, not one will stir for
the detached, the slow dickering of affect
and demise leading to the dustbin at heart.

I speak volumes across the rim of a quail.
I glisten in footage to smother all currency
and as I crumble I succeed,
empire-elect of a most honorable science,
knowing the babble that toil concludes, condones.

The Obvious Tradition

I haven't remembered anything, only that the names
and their dates have been replaced by fees
toted up out of mischief:
a whopping yellow sun, finesse swallowed hard,
a scrapbook in pantyhose dawdling beside some Shreveport-like expanse.

But now you see it, she's supposed to call.
Surely neither will converse, they merely tell,
succumbing to a disorderly shelf life like Tampax in June.
Salute the budding terminus where the East Side was.
Can there be a way to redefine the tense behind its jaunts,
the pubescent imagery a hand calls forth
as, rippling, it is thrust into the brine?

The phantom tugboat slips along
in depths past Garbo's awnings and the united glaze
which wilts, harnessing dim signatories in the windows' sarong.
Do things go further in need as I could? Or are they immune?
How else have I been taught to guess
and then been told to know, because matter equals good?
A silken light masks the entrance to the market proofs of time.

Stains of Stalin

She knew him somewhere between five p.m. and the next day.
His gaucheries were dire and nimble as iron socks.
And they rang, likewise, suppurating as
A glow along the Silk Road, as she
Healed her brow in the hospitals of a book. A stiff life
Intervening in the parlors. And then the crunch. Luncheon is served
On the patio, I kiss your hand, Madame—the era echoed
Such aggravation!—inside the thatch, the tablecloth,
Implying steely-eyed ambiguities never completely foolish enough but
Subject to derisory forced laughter brought harshly to bear
On every mother's child, as well you and I both know,
As well as the heartless, neutral, vine-colored
Slabs we put them under—
Only, angry birds that we are, I forget just which.

By Halves

do limits build
both sweet and cruel
or over to you off at
your compass studies,
visor to odd angles perforated,
plumb to sky
to service mouthful signage in pearly
cantina load where squawks from a ceiling,
headed down the demon slopes
for work place, total their sheer
carbon feed on an average night
that at any guardrail slick nails the morphological in bins?
Thus backup wealth lifts an ancient spume, glowering with grammar
whose joined bronze gives pause,
erect lapse paging glory, when wing is rag.

Clark Coolidge

Clark Coolidge was born in Providence, Rhode Island in 1939. He attended Classical High School, and then Brown University, where his father was a Professor in Music. Coolidge majored in geology, but dropped out at the end of his second year, after reading Jack Kerouac's *On the Road*, which made him realise that writing was not about finding language for a set of pre-existing ideas, but a process of discovery: 'I had thought the writer must first have it all in his head and only *then* put it into words, but no. I began to see how it was really excitingly done. You wrote from what you didn't know toward whatever could be picked up in the act.' Inspired by Kerouac's prose and the adventures of Sal Paradise and Dean Moriarty, Coolidge hitchhiked across America in the summer of 1958; in the autumn he settled in Greenwich Village, attracted by the underground writing scene – as well as the jazz. From 1960 to 1961 Coolidge worked as a bebop drummer, and his poetry often emulates the rhythm and movement of jazz. His early compositional experiments make use of cut-up and chance techniques learned from William Burroughs and John Cage, but a number also reflect his interest in geology: the poems collected in *Space* (1970), for instance, posit a metaphorical equation between words and rocks; both, Coolidge has suggested, quoting Robert Smithson's *A Sedimentation of the Mind*, 'contain a language that follows a system of splits and ruptures': 'Look at any *word* long enough,' he continues, 'and you will see it open up into a series of faults, into a terrain of particles each containing its own void.'

In the early 1970s Coolidge embarked on a series of collaborations with Tom Clark, Larry Fagin, Bernadette Mayer, and the painter Philip Guston. His work also began to prove influential on the development of what came to be known as Language poetry: in 1978 the magazine *Stations* published a symposium on Coolidge with essays by such as Charles Bernstein, Ron Silliman, and Barrett Watten, and a selection of his work featured in the first large collection of Language poetry, *In the American Tree* (1986). But Coolidge's work is, overall, less theoretically conceived and driven than that of most writers associated with the Language movement, and it shares with the poetry of Ashbery a lyrical, at times existential, sense of the fleeting, incomplete nature of its own formulations. In the final poem in this selection, 'Ashbery Explains', he fractures and expands Ashbery's minatory sonnet 'At North Farm', into a complex meditation on the implications of Ashbery's poetics, all the time reminding us that the last thing an Ashbery poem, or a Coolidge poem for that matter, will ever do is explain.

Soda Gong

box of surinam toad glass hill
pastiche bartender a live teeth
tepid tones — brine

---

orange
            milk
suction
sentence

---

do fuck they it's
               is
    you
    filled-in washtub board

---

gas viper comprende
liar snatch, unh . . .
black snake search
           tops
finger bunt I'll
flakes
    car ice in bring bong bone flat tints

Bee Elk

arch film duds
"Cheever" can aiming laps
dorm sieve

nor black   tugs toward colog
alight paramecium   bloom ice
chigger geer dads
                block

but a prime buds
Keds nor slam up labs
sham a shatter
                    puree

tins
      clock sauna
Coit ether

till sit mid sides
sign laughter
                    Anthracite

tea lure

"ounce code orange"

ounce code orange
a
      the
            ohm
trilobite trilobites

There Is a Caterpillar That Makes a Very Complicated Hammock

A hole, then the strike, on a pin buzz
the bugs are particles-of-life, pass
the clouds, a print-out on nothing,
far-away roar of the sound-whole, birds drawing
deergrass in sea swirl moundings,
I have occasion to see sky through hole in leaf,
creak. I move, I'm a relative.
Where are the snakes? the rocks?
Gray or silver, yellow or paper
birch arms and trunks, nothing but a
jet cracking air, down here among the cubist
beelike makes a stroking call
in the jello of pesters, sun through
leaf patches on rope netting
cackle, plane, divider, toad stomp along.
I've got feet slippers. I go in, sun out,
lightbulb on, phone doesn't ring,
silence while I'm out the room registers,
somewhere I'm not wood shifted an inch.
As green points the sun through an oxygen,
edges of leaves near fall, a shadow
drawing of a toe. Where's the cat.
What is a cat. Greener in his sleep than
I not in mind. Sunburn derm cooks bones
inside. I can't see my houseroof. Glass
does not exist till the birds don't, birds
don't watch. A Cessna 150 with easy carb.
I've got no idea about but write it. That
gimpy great sentence to the lawn. If
so-called green's a certain wave-length from . . .
If he called me would I hear it,
would I hear it if he called me.
A pile of logs starts up and pulls off.
A glass needle plasms through a cloud.
He had to go to great lattices to get them.
He had to stay beyond the saturday of no light.
A dome is the intermediate stage between a
needle and a liquid. "Also I've been a little
envious of you being a cloud," says Irwin

seriously. Time the skunk left us
with no yellow-jackets under kitchen window.
A flake falls at the end of the gaff afternoon.
Hairs blown on the rosin my arm is. If
I could see myself I'd be
along in the afternoon, put down in a day,
feet up in a tree, somebody about to be
calling me. A dented old plastic wading pool
upside down. Birds practicing
what is up-ended. The glass is still
what is the grass. The trunk array
behind each other. The "front of the house" is up.
Green shoot starts up and stays, blows
points, marbles elsewhere under the woods.
My lowers, my uppers, a mushroom with
an emerald green translucent cap he saw
fit to tell me, to wave away a fly pattern.
This is the writing creature under the sun
even with nothing on the mind so shouldn't
but, but do. The sky is nothing, doing nothing
and everything sounds over this line.
Imagining stringing illimitable twine
up in the sky, tree to tree, wholes,
afternoons taken, Bob Raymond and I kids
Brenton Avenue . . .

Lately I'm just going to lie here and not take pictures.

Album—A Runthru

I look in that one kind of dwindled. And in this,
look up, a truncheon in my fist, tin pot
on my head, the war. My father, I'm looking at, is my
age then and thin, his pants streak to the ground,
shadows of rosevines . . . His father sits beneath
a cat. Here the shadow has more flavor than my
trains, elbow on livingroom floor, bangs that
curl, opera broadcast, The Surreptitious Adventures of
Nightstick. I lie in the wind of the sun and hear

toots and smell aluminium smoke. The tiny oval
of my mother's youth in back and the rest is dark.
Sundays, the floor was black. At the beach, here
I'm a nest of seaweed, an earlier portrait of
surrealists I saw later, a stem of gray what
rises from my scalp. My hair is peaked in brine.
And this here hat, dark green fedora over same green
corduroy suit for a trip to the nation's capitol,
how far askance I've been since and never another
hat. Chromium rods, the hand in the guide's pocket
seems far removed. Blurry shoes on sandstone steps,
double and over exposed. Then in this one the SECRET
points to my head, shaved, and emblem, OPEN, striped
in "pirate" T-shirt and HERE IT IS. My elbow bent,
upright this time, behind a pole. I had yet to
enter at this snap the cavern beneath my sneakers.
To the right my soles protrude from beneath a boulder,
for I had trapped my mother and she asked Why.
Taken. Given. Flashlight brighter than my face,
another grotto, where the ball of twine, indirection,
gave out but we never got very far in, Connecticut.
I swim out of another cave in a further frame, cramped
gaze of sunlit days, apparel forgot. Later I reel
in a yell as my cousin takes a bite from my shank
beneath ranchhouse breezy curtains of Marion. On a trudge up
from the gasoline rockpit in the gaze of Judy Lamb,
she carries my pack, my jeans rolled as I step on
a pipe, Estwing in hand and svelte as only youthful can.
Most of those rocks remain and she married a so-so
clarinetist. My graygreen zipper jacket leans against
a concrete teepee, my father looking bullchested stands
before. Perhaps we had just argued. Central Park cement
steps of pigeons, the snow removed. Overexposed
whiteshirt at the drums, stick fingers ride cymbal
at the camera raised, livingroom Brenton with orange
& black "sea" wallpaper and orange & black tubs. I wore
a wristwatch then and never again, drumtime hitching
me past it. I graduate from highschool in white dinner
jacket and diploma and frown, too many hot shadows
back of the garage. Must roll up the bedroll with
skinny arms and lam for the caves. Dave & A. Bell by
the Ford Country Squire first time allowed alone to tool.
Bleak grass scapes of Knox farm. Rope down a crack,

mosquitoes and Koolade, sun dapple leaf moss sandwiches, ache.
Then in this group more drums on the roof, the gravel
and the flat, a cover attempt for no album even thought.
I tap and step in the dim known street. Lean on a
chimney to inhabit the sky, deep with drops. Here
I'm pressed on a wall of Tennessee limes, stones-throw
from mouth of the underground we camped in. Too many
thoughts, elide. Then lie on a beach in a doughnut
pattern shirt with a stick, a pipe?, in my mouth as my
cousin grins shiny beyond. Truro, also waiting for the
caves. With the poets then I'm fat and the driveway is
dark, the clapboards all white in a day of all talk.
This then all ends in color, my red bandana and shirt out
on Devil's Pulpit, open hand addressed to the gray
where Hawthorne and Melville now view of a highschool.
While the water still spills, and the cat squints at leaves
blown, my father wears Brahms, families lean in on one
for a group shot, and the rock remains shattered in a star.

At the Poem

You must have missed the signpost, took
the wrong turning, ended up for the sore moment
in that mud without holes. You must gaze
into the sun here to take your rest, suspend
motion and speech on a point of
zircon sand. The only articulate surfaces, they
are also somehow sounds, are buildings which
as you approach pour their facades at your feet
in a rush of the purest substances.
There are no faces to be seen since all
that is human here is you.
Numbers are become animal forms: the pounce,
the adder and the lynx. The things you loved
are all shades of moss.
Your only index the very grains of sand.
And somehow the set of things has you again,
a fascination in love of self.

On Induction of the Hand

Perhaps I've got to write better longer thinking of it as
grown up out of the same singular lost. The pattern is in, or is it
under, the hands? Better be in or it's gone from the brain
choking on airless. The outside leaves stain the sands of my
sleep even through glass and alerted in this very chair as I
thought I snoozed by the strings of this world. What world?,
evening of syntax brought full over the mounds of these what
lives but hopes. There is a wrench that a certain staring at
while balancing humours we call words in state pours wings
of edgy fondness bound useless in calm of lucidity down the
chute of the sentence. So-called duty roster activity when
typing at the seeming to be nodded at by trees. They yearn?
Saying that I am out there, with a loop I hope carries me
swaying back to here by means of them there. A tree could even
be a monad to this use, though never is it held in my heat to
be even. I let myself off myself never, no dope again trembling
my attic wires loose from their packets. Containments of such
that I never think them sendable. A poet used the word
"lozenge", he didn't write it. Some other and more careless
scribe wanted me to write one of those but the hell with what lies off
him. I remain stormy in my paradise. I pull up my pants when
the itch takes me, drops hitting page. Writing *is* a prayer for
always it starts at the portal lockless to me at last leads
to the mystery of everything that has always been written.
The state of that, trembles and then fades back in leaving
the hole where it's gone. But I pout instead of kneel. I
would rather confess, but there's no mouth to pour toward at
the poem. Perhaps it's just that the words have all been said
but not by me, and the process *is* a trial. What those leaves
are awaiting, every day my burden's finality in hand. Beneath
it are the faces I've yet to replace in a rock as stern and fluid as
Piero's Christless blue. But all the while I eye you, demon,
your bird hoards are clustering here. Sent for calm and
brought crazy still.

One of Essence's Entrances

The blame of the day comes knotted in the pad of night
Sieves of the blotters we obey are throttled in copy
Are they standards these holes of boast in slanted rhyme
Strident forth that lets the lips and frees the core from care

A lap I have seized on tongs arcaded acts in turn
Such gaff that the throat is bent and strings with harm
Drop over the decimal fence come felt to true
Make of chime in the chalked-up trailings avoided

A liver beats too in this brain rose
Thrown back in shivers on the launch of song
A twisted thus married burn that leaves that touch
Hauled off in brace of themes that break before

I head no solid avenue braves the flood
I sign no echo of conduits sieve my blood

Darkling Thrums

What so true as night come fused
So shown to glance the brain off plumb
It lights the well dull thought enthused
Envelops dim a light to sum

I hold it throttled to engage
The world in shadow state as bend
The threading things the sight enrage
The climbers inch in scorn to end

So this has passed, this shuttered heat
That cluttered nightscape at the heart
A shade mere memory of the start
The brain erases to complete
As shells then buckle in their rate
All night rings lurkful rage contort

A Dalliance with Salt Sides

Gents bounce thoroughly around in turn-of-the-century
costumes, and cartwheels of parasols, primrose proportions.
Hulot there tampering with lids. He thinks
all this dally is a matter of fact. Like the chair
slat of the ship shape *should*
collapse into flats at this same point of
beach each time. But no one matters
about him. A cast of gray face
in the morning day. The flue cats smile.
Everyone is composed with striped pens.
Chattering at the seal of the umbrella bones.
As if Trouville were slotted Malibu
and the gray ghosts of its there. Boudin
dolloping by, in a sealing wax raiment.
Pardon, mon Boulevardier. Na beef, sah?
Close that thatched door! And the collies
drop rolling out of the hunt huts. Slow
revolving propeller beach, with the porch
at its knees. Got trouble bends? Send 'em
up in a kite balloon. Knowledge of the
nodular sort brine in Hulot's mind.
As he folds the stubble into a semblance picnic.
He parades the patrol in prepeppered lozenges.
Silly but ordered munching in larval but
sophisticate cupolas. "I'd have the nerve if
I'd learned that word." Kings of Castles
loose in the sand mine, lighting orange
baboons at the sun. Cement has expressly
yet to be invented, or still not so pressed
into use. Carnivals can still be of sand alone,
and out of fog. Hulot discusses anchors with
the Trellis King. He has memorized his
glasses and laces them on the dog. Then
it is told that chickens need his permit.
Somebody ups and pastes a celluloid of monkeys
on the central sphere salt seller. Now
a biplane or elevated candy sack. An
entrance to the Told Elves' Pickets lining
any calibration of brain at all. Huzzah!
Dog dug hole under Hulot! Much marching

grain fun. His magic dives laughing inward.
Whose thought suspends his throat? Throngs
shocked at what the Dago ate. As gingered
as if he had whipped the Pimpernell.
A cast of cobras coiling back the dunes.
Hulot serves.

On the Road

Well, you just have to read and get involved
with things and scribble. The letters
under the mountain, and the wrath that
turns auto. We'll never sour up any
plans by jabbering on. We'll whittle
while we run. And in back of it all
the spiral ramp of conversations, higgly-
piggling over hours and starts and landings.
Nobody digs it all better than in
comminglings of flowage, hot off the rocks
back of the batter pen where dimers stand.
And the flash floats out of the stars into
our upraised tips. Writing means motion.
The hover left behind in the lever jacket,
the car park flap, the inhabited sever.
I was ready to take up amazement and
follow the words.

"He walked around and couldn't think of anything"

He walked around and couldn't think of anything.
Nothing had been put back. Later he would think
of all the names and they would bother him.
But right now everything was empty. The world
rose and fell, everything beating in regular
parentheses. Even the light, a pulsing gray.
He lifted a hand and then put it back, down.
By his side was a lift, which he entered and
shut the doors. He stood inside not moving
for a long time, listening to everything
without a thought.

Fragments are our wholes.

Ashbery Explains

The people on the next block over from yours, you know?
Sounds transduced from ceiling to ceiling
to thought that won't admit of a washer replaced
without dousing all and sundry in sand and a mild solution
of pinks and reeds, hard sodium, the cap off the tube
he stood and he said, and he lay long and he thought
his mind encompassed, his perimeter taken in a bit
everybody talking at once but only one thread assorted
from it all a parrot reproduced on call

Out on a rooftop head down timing the sun
wishing it hadn't all come easy to such a rinse
living in a chipper vacuum of donuts chatting and jotting
and walking and salting the numbers coming up on the surface
of a silky phone, how can you store
all the bones of one time a leavening for
the canceled strikes in bridled strokes
I pick a pen from room of cobbled stacks
and head for Mars, Saturn

Add the epithet "farm," north and to the sum of that place
and you have the counting drama, away from which we reside but not
as anonymous kinds, drops of the goblin into the proper reservoir
it would be bogus continuing just to continue nonetheless
renders us very much against the day hell became a lover
of the spinal stanzas, he came, he didn't grow there
by the act of remaining there, mortal and hatless
strolled right down into the river the message takes
reason is plenty and we stake our obligations on it
but not our sayings, those tremble in a wind of
the reminding of focus, or a difficult shadow of
a pretty death, one's arm contrasts with any
of several reactive poems, ones taken up now but
not yet broken into, the clearest brush
will line the ledge with a conscious magic and absolve us
ink at an end and later on that day

Perhaps the he he is is
not explainable by the you you
have always mixed feelings with
the identity a gloomy and barren place for
a metaphor, the first field or last vice
or stanza containing dish or fish or sky
running with milk, or dots to the end
then dash and the initials responsible

A poem is larger than the situation
of one held longer than it actually is
though plenty would just continue
the salt charred under a lamp arm or
low sun the review couldn't be bothered with
one feeling ever borne out since its origin?
but close enough to the line if you are
the right person playing it or messenger
casting aside the bay leaf for death with a difference

Here and now Captain Specific is staring placidly
at an object
to an absolute halt, wrapping yard and sky
in needlework and frosting, binding energy
on the vastness of a stall
but he cannot reveal it
has not the language for it, is
unable to receive a thing

Gradually substances pall beyond the perimeter
the tin mine is rotting in honey
the strew of loam edges toward the oceans
the alleys echo themselves sour, clattering ink falls
toads clear the earth, it is perhaps
little enough that the fish of chalk is regained in light
that no thought is wasted on everything
everywhere and not at all in sole declension

But the poem prefers death and milk in contrasting stanzas
and now that I am here I feel it is all about
simply living, not looking for something else
the miles marked up on the trunks, or anything lucid
that anyone objectively drops, these or suitably ringing
others are mates to my nut's fattening, stated
the harmful chap pleasantly who just shared your most
recent and addling repast, he is the one to ask
the graduate who stands just outside the palace of remedies
and asks himself another for every one of yours
constant piecemeal and won't budge

Charles North

Charles North was born in Brooklyn in 1941, and grew up in and around New York City. He studied English and philosophy at Tufts, English at Columbia, and then, briefly, law at Harvard. He began writing in his mid-twenties. Like Joseph Ceravolo and Bill Berkson, North attended Kenneth Koch's New School poetry workshop, which introduced him to the work of Ashbery, Schuyler, O'Hara, and Koch himself, and to that of their favoured European modernists, Mayakovsky, Lorca, Henri Michaux, and Francis Ponge, among others. North's first collection, *Lineups* (1972), was inspired by Rimbaud's 'Voyelles', but rather than attributing a set of colours to the vowels of the alphabet, North used baseball lineups (catcher, pitcher, shortstop and so on) to create 'teams' of movies, diseases, cities, vegetables, and parts of the body. Like much of his subsequent work, the concept of *Lineups* allows us to ponder, indeed revel in, 'ideas of order', to borrow a phrase from Wallace Stevens, without having to believe such orders are inevitable or immutable.

A wry, poised playfulness often operates just below the surface of North's poetry. James Schuyler characterised his wit as 'metaphysical', and compared it with that of Marvell in being 'not satirical, but informed with pity'. His best work reveals also, one might argue, a Marvellian delicacy of perception and sensitivity to the nuances of language and genre, gently entangling the reader in weird, thought-provoking conundrums ('Nothing grows out of nothing / Into a spidery realism'), and absurd but delightful literary conceits – as when he invents a Dorothy Wordsworth-style journal entry that uncannily anticipates Yeats's 'Sailing to Byzantium' ('Lunch was pleasant, we were given a choice of fish, flesh or fowl. William had mackerel . . .'), or fabricates a lyrical cento from the stirring clichés of Robert W. Service. Like Ashbery, North invites us to peer around the edges of genres and idioms, but also induces an amused, buoyant self-consciousness that allows us to relax inside the limitations of whatever conventions his poetry invokes. North has also evolved a sophisticated style of poetic meditation on which William Cowper, to whom he pays tribute in 'For a Cowper Paperweight', may have been an influence. Ruminative poems like 'Eye Reflecting the

Gold of Fall' and 'The Year of the Olive Oil' certainly deliver what he calls in the Cowper poem 'the pleasure of the low key / and mastery of cadence', as their precise but elegantly slanted formulations unfurl according to some elusive but imperturbable logic. Such poems encourage us to feel adequate 'to life's daily immensities', and accept with grace and imagination the minor dilemmas and major uncertainties that North's poetry tracks so accurately, and converts into a beautifully scored paean to imaginative freedom.

Elizabethan & Nova Scotian Music

What will see us through, a certain calm
Born of the willingness to be not cowed
The begonia idea of the universe
And because life is so short
A way of being unfaithful like the tide
Minus its characteristic awareness.

Moving is the world and all its creatures
Known by the things that surround it
Love, money, titles, the periphrastic way
Of being other than we are not
Throughout the long afternoon of language
Attractive though dead, such calm falling

And issuing in a well-meant spiel
Involving money as a metaphor: Money is
The only metaphor and because life is short
A gross keyboard of light and sometimes strength
As well to be aware of its fickleness
As stab it in the back with gentleness.

The Pastoral

Now the body is the body's flower
And the head revolves in a whirl
Of false judgment, the breath
Of a camel cast inside a date

Those fingers knead a furtive cake
The cost of labor which was life
Is passed down in the form of heat
Which we resemble in letting it out

Meanwhile the crow of responsibility
Is perfected, as in the pastoral:
Nothing grows out of nothing
Into a spidery realism

A Few Facts About Me

I am moved often, and easily
without knowing why or finding it appropriate
to be a consequence of somebody else's unfathomable will.

I can be taken in by the suggestion of emotion in others
even if their actions are as foreign to human psychology
as the emotions of European children in American textbooks

or American textbooks in American life. Deciding what my life
will be has always been the decision as to what it has been,
and before I met you I knew what it would be like, and planned to be in the
    path

of whatever could change it, whether or not it prevented me
from being the sole translator of your natural eloquence.
As the captain of my fate and steerer of my star

I don't find any single decision irrevocable,
feeling inadequate to life's daily immensities, a condition
of the unwillingness to act, for of the things that are human

the best is to be unavoidable, which doesn't make it any better
but doesn't make it worse—like that sunset I'm always refusing to look behind
or away from as if to be dull were the reverse of not shining

and living selfishly when that too is exhaustible.

Eye Reflecting the Gold of Fall

Silver is the ruby's faded glare
Awkward silence taking it out to sea
And you away. The morning
Is its own highway, interleaded
With ears at the important points,
Each the size of a key of typewriter type.
To hornets we are all electroencephalographically
Neutral. Everyone is speaking jargon, especially
The ducks which look orange in this light;—
Sunny as a fruit tree, or as a lime drawn
From the tops of the fruit trees to the telephone wire
Dividing the ocean, whose neck is the horizon.
Some words ("like 'fuck'") require objects some of the time; others
Are content to be themselves, suspended like a chair,
Covered in green ink. Everyone's comet
Strikes the earth, in a way.
The birds stay where they are, stretching to get the birdseed
Until they resemble the clothesline, white
With a dark shimmer. Half-cocked, except for a hay
Riding the air, the sky pushed branches against a screen
Where some T-shirts have caught, drying in powder
That will make them stiff and fragrant. As sound is released
By the head in front, the back of the neck
In back, and out and beyond the honking.
Everyone sleeps at least part of the time, the pilot
In the plane, the oceanographer in the bathysphere,
The judge on the bench, everyone else between eating and
Going to the bathroom, the window pouring
It through like the boat.
Some of the harvest words are
Also used for hunting, making them doubly unresonant,
Like an agglutinative language
Condensed to a single word, unspoken; or
The moon with no breath on it, touching your forehead in a complete
Absence of what meteorologists call weather
In a country on the verge of capitulating
To its smallest city. One would steer
Carefully to the south towards the lighthouse.
Slowly the lawn quiets down.
Each berry is a species of robin, all inflect night

Like the ocean's rush over a bumpy road. As the radio
Spars with air, random to the space it occupies
To the inclusion of skin. Not the argument
From design since there are no stars to push, but thin
Points of maroon beside some gold
Letters which thud, far
Out of their cosmological depth.
Then the berries leave the trees;
The birds chase them, delivered to a prior spot where each,
Like the ocean, is inflated and simplified,
Marooned no more than late afternoon mist dispensed
From an apple tree claiming to be the air outside the room,
Supporting everything in it. In the turtle's mouth.
The turtle looks up. Trees and grass, chairs and clouds,
Sit in the middle of the lawn, the snowy lawn of the air.
With a breeze the ocean stutters, in the middle of
Mumbling. But the ship is already a blur,
Each point created for the benefit of others
Which react to it as if it were poison ivy, catching the same spray.
A chorus steps out of the spray. Two, in fact;
Astonished at not having made themselves known before,
With brandied snow, burning eyelashes.
You are the hotel, but you are also
The vandal, as well as the house detective.
Every spray accelerates, stops, so you can watch it;
Banging like grain like the door against ice air.

For Dorothy Wordsworth

After an early breakfast we hoisted sail, preferring to confront the falls in better weather. Within the space of an hour it grew black and thundered so mightily we thought the surface of the water would crack! We took refuge at the singing school . . . There were students everywhere at work and at play, some at instruments, some at their song, the young in one another's arms like birds in the trees, entirely unmindful of our presence. Lunch was pleasant, we were given a choice of fish, flesh or fowl. William had mackerel . . . The dishwasher was the sort to pass unnoticed in a crowd, nonetheless, he caught our attention. For he had hung his tattered coat upon a stick and sang to himself, every so often clapping his hands and singing louder as he saw us watching him, as if to say a man is a paltry thing unless he has music in his soul. Over the fireplace hung an inexpensive tile fashioned to look like gold mosaic. The fire danced, gyrated, inexpressible; in its movement it seemed to create objects of air, and then to retrieve them as one might replace gold jewels in their box. As we sat by the fire I couldn't help feeling that if I had had the control of my destiny, like a lord or a lady the "emperor of my body," I might have remained in that sensual atmosphere all summer long. The evening passed pleasantly among reflections on the day, the past few days, and the days that were to come.

Sunrise with Sea Monster

Well, we either do it or we don't, as the pigeon said to the loaf of bread
doubling as the sky, that is, unaffectedly rocky and clay gray, the color of rocks
bordering but not reflecting oceans and in particular the one that finds its way
here
every so often, though not right now; a function of light and surface qualities
such as polish, facet, regularity of design,
implied or announced mineral content, the ability to stand still in a storm,
and those qualities that enter surface and suffuse it, or melt suddenly
into the next door apartment building, swept down into the back garden tow,
like transitions whether in writing or in music that aren't really transitional
so that cadence is a matter, ordinarily, of being stunned rather than construed,
but no diminishment, as in "fancy" and "open fifths" and "environmental
sweepstakes"

The Year of the Olive Oil

for Yuki Hartman

I sing the olive oil, I who lately sang
The clarinets in their sturdy packing case, the failure
Of the economy to be both seasonal and self-sufficient,
Packed off like cargo ships into the dim asperities of twilight.
Spread on Italian bread it became the summer sky—
And sometimes (brittle as failure) as musical as crystal.
One bottle contained all the arts. Another stimulated conversation
Which was itself the first pressing.
Darker pressings for the night
And each dawn had its geographical nuances, French and Spanish
Greek and Syrian, as on overcast days there were lumps
Of tough, overworked dough, gray and suffocating, with just a trace of gloss.
Then success was measured in thinness like an expensive watch;
Failures were as muddy as colors mixed by an infant.
Even virtual sewing machine oil, rancid with use, had a place
Beside winters when spears of sunlight, like armed tears,
Fenced in flame-blue iris and more ingenious pupil.
There were kingdoms advertising their future connections

(In crystal palaces with silver flags, cork-like minarets)
Fields of long, slender wheat coated with spring rain:
Sharing with the Jams the flow of shade
And with the Glues and Ointments a calculator-like display
Of the forces of temperature and pressure, as on August days in city office
buildings.
One type was restricted to the human body, as its perfection and condiment.
Before this, there would have been no adhesive
For the world scrape, no solution (admittedly fugitive).
Music caught in the throat like peanut butter
And chords were torn apart, something like peaceful war resisters
Until there was little sense of connection.
People read and wrote in fits, misunderstanding the true nature of the medium.
Then or soon after the intellect was felt to be
A part of life's suspension, and barbers never had to oil
Their scissors. If there was an occasional
Domestic squabble, it ran to gentle advice.
It is clear that vegetables, as in Andrew Marvell, were the chief
Image and model of human desire; and like water off a duck's back
—Pressed to golden brown, with pale gold juices intact and *no* fat—
Slid the momentary chagrins and anxieties, the bankruptcies
Spiritual and otherwise—otherwise irremediable; except for
Long slow decanting like passages of pure virgin time.
They had, as far as I can see, no word for friction.
It looked like a partial though real changeover to ball bearings
On the part of even the most adamant faculties of mind and body,
Writer's cement block and fractious self-interest group (the quiet ferment
Made clear by the necessity to be glass-clad, stoppered)
Enabling human achievement to flourish like a gold breeze,
Circular and reforming in the glow and liquid fragment.

The Postcard Element in Winter

1

Supposing the wildlife became a person
who suddenly sprouted into an infinite number of ideas
each idea casting an ideal glow from canyon to canyon
like the most wandering star space

whose atmosphere singes the very park—
as though the city existed to be barreled through
in spite of the windy quiet on its face
the factory snap, the raw potatoes and practicing the bassoon

2

~~Your recent letter is so stupid so utterly moronic its~~
~~a little difficult to believe it was~~
~~written by a human being let alone someone~~
~~who made it past the second grade you~~
~~miserable bastard do you eat~~
~~from a plate~~ thanks for your letter of January 5th
I enjoyed getting it

For a Cowper Paperweight

Not that his writing isn't moving when
it doesn't seem it should be,
owing in part, at least, to the cloud of difficulty
surrounding his difficult life,
the pleasure of the low key
and mastery of cadence—but that it is
difficult to say why some of it
should be as good as it is, the life
of the writing apart from the life.
The quiet assertions made,
assertion becomes an extended lyric

which, foregoing rapture (as it foregoes
rhapsody) presents feeling in such
a way that it ascends human heights,
both detailing and depending on
the level motion of the feeling tone,
like a long headline broken up into
individual letters and presented
at random, one letter at a time
throughout long and occasionally tedious
narrative and description, the promise of sunshine
throughout a long brightly overcast afternoon.
(As though—almost—one had to compete
with the weather and lose in order
to feel anything, or as though mere utterance
blended one with what was being uttered,
in this case ground and sky, the nature
and numerous pleasures of being between.)
Nor do the exceptions in what prevails,
"I was a stricken deer, that left the herd
Long since; with many an arrow deep infixt
My panting side was charg'd," alter
the weather of the context, while lending a sense
of extra, unrepressed life to the whole;
to a whole consisting of dullness
as well as all the other neighboring kingdoms.
A sense that pleasure is often
pleasure of recognition which doesn't depend
on prior experience—though one has had that too.
"Oh Winter, ruler of th'inverted year,
Thy scatter'd hair with sleet like ashes fill'd,
Thy breath congeal'd upon thy lips, thy cheeks
Fring'd with a beard made white with other snows
Than those of age, thy forehead wrapt in clouds,
A leafless branch thy sceptre, and thy throne
A sliding car, indebted to no wheels,
But urg'd by storms along its slipp'ry way,
I love thee, all unlovely as thou seem'st,
And dreaded as thou art!"

The Dawn

The dawn was contagious, spreading rapidly about the heavens.
Flann O'Brien

TO BE

Immortal.

ONLY

A pencil line of sunlight is climbing
Straight up the chimney, stopping about two inches
From the top

IMPINGING

On a template of powder blue without end

IT FOLLOWS THAT

Compressed, highlighted and seductively polished
Within a naturally limited theater of operations
Snow or sleet, the occasional burst rising to produce
A new century

SPACE IS FURIOUS

Still beneath the roof of your hair
The dials keynote our penchant for constructing
Problems that test the ground underneath, reflecting wintergreen
All the way up to buildings including several different varieties

THE WAY IT PRODDED

All nabis and all
Oily charm, conveniently summarized
Which is not to say without vague hopes of escape into the evening sky

PARTICULARLY THE DAWN

Approximately fifteen feet back from where
The houses, secure at least temporarily from flattening,
Peered out over what had been left of the horizon—that is,
What hadn't been previously usurped
By the "developers"

WHEN LAST WE

Met.

EVEN NOW

Your arms are the unencumbered coastline

LIKE AN ALTO SAXOPHONE

With cherries in the bell. It isn't
Selected cities

LIMNING

And individuating green light; as though some passing cloud

SOFTER THAN LASERS TO STYROFOAM

Not exactly carried aloft like the anthem of autumn
But a rubric of sopping wet air that
Has aimed its complement in a forthcoming way

A SWEET SMELL

Like the armpit
Of an angel

OR PERFECTION OF THE LIFE

The earth is
Pulled up to the surface, or
The surface is pulled down till it hits; either way
The blue is spooned over lush

WHY I AM NOT A GERMAN ROMANTIC

THE PLACE OF RUNNING BOARDS

If, and it's a big one,
This clumsy desire to be confined to you and you only
Means hammering out the decision
Where all is difficult to see

AS THOUGH EACH FRAGRANT CAUSEWAY

Doubled the space between monsters—I mean trampling
The news from the perspective of summer
Until the only boarder of note sheds quality
In the form of clothespins pushed up towards the thinnest leaf

NOT BEING OR BEING NOT BEING

The primroses

OF MY DISCONTENT

Not the shoal
Where we argue the limitless side, but somehow
Swarming down the coal chute to be played
According to those golden notions of equal
And opposite reaction, swallowed up by, at least
In part, the same religious architecture
That works on the mind like feelers, extending even into the current

LIKE CARROTS TO HILLS

The gray carrots, and the almost
Maple rolling hills

Detail

Actually the idea of representing
putting one foot where the other
can't possibly go has always
seemed fragile at best
            and as for *this*
            standing in for always,
            the rowboat funding serpentine
            darknesses, even what won't
            change can't be said to be
            other than it looks like
            to us as we account for it,
            leaving the position of auditor
not to say guarantor up for grabs like
stars on a windy night, and any and all
vestiges of allegiance in tracks made
by snowshoes, of by and for the moment's loss

Words from Robert W. Service

The things you had no right to do, the things you should have done,
Of cities leaping to stature, of fame like a flag unfurled
And a city all a-smoulder and . . . as if it really mattered.
And the greasy smoke in an inky cloak went streaking down the sky.

It sort of made me think a bit, that story that you told
All glamour, grace and witchery, all passion verve and glow,
The all-but-fluid silence,—yet the longing grows and grows.
Now wouldn't you expect to find a man an awful crank!

For the debit side's increasing in a most alarming way
From the vastitudes where the world protrudes through clouds like seas
    up-shoaled.
So the stranger stumbles across the room, and flops down there like a fool
Dreaming alone of a people, dreaming alone of a day.

The Wanderlust has haled me from the morris chairs of ease
By the darkness that just drowns you, by the wail of home desire.
It's also true I longed for you and wrote it on an egg . . .
Though where I don't exactly know, and don't precisely care.

It seems it's been since the beginning; it seems it will be to the end
To hit the high spots sometimes, and to let your chances slip.
For the lake is yonder dreaming, and my cabin's on the shore.
In the little Crimson Manual it's written plain and clear:

We're merely "Undesirables," artistic more or less,
The people ever children, and the heavens ever blue,
Dear ladies, if I saw you now I'd turn away my face
Oh, the clammy brow of anguish! the livid, foam-flecked lips!

I'm not so wise as the lawyer guys, but strictly between us two
I'm the Steinway of strange mischief. We're all brutes more or less.
Then you've a hunch what the music meant . . . hunger and night and the stars.
All honey-combed, the river ice was rotting down below.

Landscape & Chardin

I have to confess that *Bon appétit* never strikes me as an appropriate invitation. It seems too . . . medicinal, like charging a poem with the obligation to improve, or at least define, one's sense of self. Speaking of which, how many of our great poets are themselves more than 8% of the time? Not just the obvious cases. Take Yeats. Or take Hart Crane. Take almost anyone. I don't feel as confident saying so, but I'm pretty sure the same is true for painters even if the percentages go up some. So much of what we experience as present is earmarked for the future. Sing, Contingency, of a single membrane in the process of becoming a frame house open to the charcoal and cantaloupe of evening—of the unfavored nation status of line. I like the idea that the air is too close to either prove or disprove its existence, and that it has no stake whatever in the issue. The deer are practically pets. A few days ago, the small one that lay down to die got up when no one was looking. No one ever sees a live skunk, yet we take the facts of its life on the evidence. Along with a certain amount of shivering and pure, or at least uncharacterizable, *qualia.* The impressions planted before the realms collide. Still, the houses, linear or not, retain a humanity despite their continuity with anything and everything, power and phone lines as much as faraway loosestrife whose color (whatever else it may take cover under) floods the eye. The pond calmed down earlier. Written on in only a few spots apart from the questionable egrets—living question marks is what I mean. I don't, personally, see much suffering other than the everpresent kind. I can envision the Incredible Shrinking Man, by now not so incredible, up to his neck in ground cover or the dried up stalks showing above the pond surface, barely taking in the postings against deer-hunting, the freeze-frames of the hawks, the occasional ghostly flock of wild turkeys among the ubiquitous cedars—plus hints of yet-to-be-instantiated structure. The lintels, what there is of them, are heartbreaking.

Ron Padgett

Ron Padgett was born in 1942 in Tulsa, Oklahoma, where he attended public schools. He has described his childhood in Tulsa in an evocative memoir entitled 'Among the Blacks', published alongside his translation of Raymond Roussel's seminal short story, 'Parmi les noirs', and in greater depth in his memoir of his father, *Oklahoma Tough*. His father lived mainly by bootlegging, though he also dealt in second-hand cars. While still in high school Padgett co-founded with Joe Brainard and Dick Gallup a magazine, *The White Dove Review*, which attracted contributions from Allen Ginsberg, Jack Kerouac, Robert Creeley, and LeRoi Jones, as well as from the poet who would become the fourth member of the Tulsa Four, Ted Berrigan. Padgett moved to New York in 1960 to study English and Comparative Literature at Columbia; there he came under the influence of Kenneth Koch, and as editor of *Columbia Review* caused a scandal by attempting to publish a poem by Berrigan the authorities deemed obscene because it contained the word *fuck*. Padgett studied in Paris on a Fulbright Fellowship during the academic year 1965–6, and the translations he has subsequently published of Apollinaire, Duchamp, Cendrars and Reverdy reveal the impact on his own development of a certain strand of experimental French poetry. He has also, as Director of St Mark's Poetry Project (1978–80) and then Publications Director of the Teachers & Writers Collaborative, which promotes innovative ways of teaching imaginative writing to children, been among the most active disseminators of New York School poetry to the world at large.

Padgett is a prolific writer whose work radiates an infectious delight in the unexpected, the goofy, the implausible, in whatever disrupts our expectations and pushes us to consider new possibilities and conjunctions. He was one of the first poets to introduce aspects of the aesthetic of Pop Art into poetry, as for instance in a sonnet inspired by Andy Warhol's movie *Sleep*, which consists of the line 'Zzzzzzzzzzzzzzzzzzzzzzzzzz' repeated fourteen times. But Padgett has never allowed his poetry to be dominated by a particular set of concepts or theories, and his enthusiasm for collaboration (his and Berrigan's *Bean Spasms* was published in 1968, and he has also often worked with painters such as Brainard and Jim Dine), suggests the importance to him of subjecting his own imaginative impulses to forces beyond his control. His poems are full of characters who suddenly erupt into the narrative, like Tommy and Mr Bushwanger in 'Famous Flames', of surreally reworked stories like that of the three bears ('Prose Poem'), of bizarre locutions and exclamations ('—Bgawk!' opens 'Poem for El Lissitzky'), of volatile dreamscapes that dissolve or recede, or suddenly come starkly into focus, opening our senses to the space and climate of the present.

Joe Brainard's Painting "Bingo"

I suffer when I sit next to Joe Brainard's painting "Bingo"

I could have made that line into a whole stanza

I suffer
When I sit
Next to Joe
Brainard's painting
"Bingo"

Or I could change the line arrangement

I suffer when I sit

That sounds like hemorrhoids
I don't know anything about hemorrhoids
Such as if it hurts to sit when you have them
If so I must not have them
Because it doesn't hurt me to sit
I probably sit about $\frac{8}{15}$ of my life

Also I don't suffer
When I sit next to Joe Brainard

Actually I don't even suffer
When I sit next his painting "Bingo"
Or for that matter any of his paintings

In fact I didn't originally say
I suffer when I sit next to Joe Brainard's painting "Bingo"
My wife said it
In response to something I had said
About another painting of his
She had misunderstood what I had said

Louisiana Perch

Certain words disappear from a language:
their meanings become attenuated,
grow antique, insanely remote or small,
vanish.
                    Or become something else:
transport. Mack
the truck driver falls for a waitress
    where the water flows. The

great words are those without meaning:
    from a their or
    Or the for a the
    The those

The rest are fragile, transitory
    like the waitress, a

beautiful slender young girl!
I love her! Want to
marry her! Have hamburgers!
Have hamburgers! Have hamburgers!

Ode to Bohemians

1

The stars at night
Are big and bright
The moon above
A pale blue dove

The trees bent out
By windy shout
Of West Wind god
And the soldiers bolted from their ranks

—Did they o did they?—

And spilled across the countryside,
ants escaping some ant doom,
the final trumpet from the god of ant death . . .

while their wives were waiting in the kitchen doorway
in red aprons and yellow bandanas,
really beautiful little black ants . . .

2

Two eyes bulging out with red lines
and rolling upon the ground . . .
all the better to see you with,
microscopic weakling!
You rush below the microscopes of government,
the government of Russia, the government of the U.S.A.,
the horrible governments of Argentina and Brazil, the suspicious
governments of Greece, Venezuela and Turkey,
the governments strong and weak, a few weird bigshots
making you eat dirt and like it, buddy.
For me, I say, "Fuck it."
I have a glass of red wine
and a beret upon my head,
I am tipsy in Montmartre,
my smock smeared with paint
and the lipstick of script girls,
and I salute zees life I lead,
O happy vagabond! O stalwart bohemian,
defying the ordinary rules of society
to express your inner self,
to tell those callous motherfuckers
what it's like, to achieve
the highest glory of man
and then sink back in its clouds
never to be seen again, like strange celebrities
whose caricatures grow dim and fade
from the pages of memory. Thank you, anyway,
you colorful individuals.

Famous Flames

With all my faults
I do have one virtue:
I respect the idea of the noble book.
(No kidding!)
I take seriously the works of Aristotle,
although I do not usually like them.
I take seriously the *Tao Teh Ching*
and I always bark like a dog,
with the gray silhouette of a factory
against a deep red sky
and it is the France of Zola,
he whose high heels clicked
against a marble bust of Pallas.
These gentlemen are very interesting.
Take Montaigne. A peculiar guy, and
very interesting. Or Spinoza,
he of the face ugly
and geometry as divinity.
He looked in the mirror and said, "Ouch!"
and he looked into the ouch
and saw a perfect circle.
A leads to B and to C
and that explains the universe!
Unfortunately that face belonged to René Descartes!

Me, I bit into the coleslaw
and killed the dragon where he breathed
funny fumes on the pages of Literature.
"I am Everyman."
What a funny thing to say!
Would a tree say, "I am tree"?
I do not think so,
I do not think so just yet.

An ominous sensation steals over the back
as though a magnetic field
were searching, vaguely,
for another magnetic field.
Card players, in marathon games,
smoking Camels, have claimed
to have seen visions, one
in which the Virgin Mary came down
out of the sky and gave him the three of spades.
Others believe they can change the pips
by force of mind, as the card flies through the air,
and it's your open.
You sit at the present moment
with the future ready to welcome you,
until the bubble bursts
and the crowds begin to move again.
It is Christmas, 1944. The man
who invented the question mark
was laughing in heaven. Human beings
had turned into exclamation points
that threw skinny shadows across the earth
as it turned in space lit only by an old flashlight.
It was a pretty cheap production,
and when Tommy entered it in the science fair
Mr. Bushwhanger was embarrassed.
He ran and banged his head
against the wall of the faculty lounge
until his glasses fell on the floor,
burst into flame.

Early Triangles

Can you feel the swell—
or is there one?—
of something vast & wonderful
coming over America?
Or is that just the glow
of lights from Montpelier?
I stood out in the woods
and spoke to the trees with their leaves,
and they answered back. They said,
"Jerome, Jerome,
return to your village."
I did so, and began
to lick postage stamps.
Red ones and green ones, some
with pink and yellow,
delicate triangles in the afternoon.

Blue Bananas

First came Patchen,
then Ferlinghetti,
the giraffe has a long neck,
I live in a house.
It is warm in the rooms and cold out,
but they cannot utter a sound
and you have a big mouth!
I put on my bus driver's costume
and sputter around the apartment
as chateaux fall across the sea,
the First World War, you know,
with the champagne of Rheims
fizzing underground while *des obus*
sailed through a Beethoven dream
in which he is surrounded by
statues of Muddy Waters.

There should be hundreds of statues
of Muddy Waters in the front lawns
of every home in America, all wired
to belt out his various hits, such as
"Tiger in Your Tank," "Hoochie Coochie Man,"
and "Moonlight in Vermont." In Vermont
and "Moonlight in Vermont" people are stirring
large bowls of soup in which some trees
are reflected, green images on red steam.
Picasso placed some blue bananas
on the table—it was green—but hey,
they really were blue those bananas,
harvested in South America by bright blue insects
that wear glasses and are seen
through prisms when the electrical charges
of the brain generate enough magnetism
to pull the whole system into an ellipse.
I told you I had a big mouth.

Second Why

I have always found Mark Twain to be a rather depressing character, especially in movies about him, and I have always avoided his books like the plague, hated even the titles; but why? He's like me, with whom I have this love-hate relationship! The psychoanalyst rose from his desk and approached with his trim gray

beard. "Young man,"

he said gravely, "you have nothing
to fear. Float now, out the door,
on a river of electrical confidence,
and give off sparks, and be a sign,
and when you will have gone
they will say, 'Jesus! what a guy!'"
Some clouds left the sky

and its blue was purer. It
was a lovely deep baby buggy
into which the universe had plunged,
happy and innocent as a baby
going goo-goo and its mother's
lovely legs crisscrossing in the afternoon,
with the light through the trees
the way it used to be in 1948,
so primitive but beautiful in a stark
sort of presentation, pine
trees clustered at the Cozy Pines Motel
where the dim pink neon is restful
and the prices are reasonable,
sane, civilized, benevolent.

High Heels

I have a vision
in my head of Cubism
and Constructivism
in all their artistic purity
joined with a decorative attractiveness
that exceeds deliciousness,
even more to be desired
than becoming a milkman
in a white suit and hat
delivering milk to the back door
of a white frame house
on a street lined with elms
and being invited inside
by the curvaceous, translucent lady
of the house, not once
but many times, too many times,
perhaps, for later her husband
will be coming home
with a sledgehammer in his hand,
the pink hand with light blue fingernails, oh
you have colored the wrong picture!
You were to put the pink and blue
on the beachball on the next page.

Poem for El Lissitzky

—Bgawk!
There goes that Polly again!

The big storybook closed
and it was bedtime for real . . .
all little children go to bed now,
and sleep you well inside your pajamas,
and let your dreams rise softly
as the bubbles on the decal
over the headboard

by which you sleep
your wooden sleep,
little wooden children
with ragged edges
that must be sanded.
Time is the sandpaper—
isn't that original?

"Time is the sandpaper,"
I said as the housewife
opened her door to me.
I was selling vacuum cleaners door-to-door.
Once they let me in
I sweet-talked them into the bedroom,
where once again I said,
"Time is the sandpaper."
This time they swooned.
Never did sell many vacuum cleaners, though.

Love Poem

We have plenty of matches in our house.
We keep them on hand always.
Currently our favorite brand is Ohio Blue Tip,
though we used to prefer Diamond brand.
That was before we discovered Ohio Blue Tip matches.
They are excellently packaged, sturdy
little boxes with dark and light blue and white labels
with words lettered in the shape of a megaphone,
as if to say even louder to the world,
"Here is the most beautiful match in the world,
its one and a half inch soft pine stem capped
by a grainy dark purple head, so sober and furious
and stubbornly ready to burst into flame,
lighting, perhaps, the cigarette of the woman you love,
for the first time, and it was never really the same
after that. All this will we give you."
That is what you gave me, I
become the cigarette and you the match, or I
the match and you the cigarette, blazing
with kisses that smoulder toward heaven.

Light as Air

1

It's calm today. I sit outside, or inside by the window, and look out, and for a moment I realize my left hand is holding up my head. I see the light on everything, trees, hills, and clouds, and I do not see the trees, hills, and clouds. I see the light, and it plays over my mind that it is any day, not today, just day.

2

The wind is making the trees swoosh and the volume goes up and down. I have been sitting here for some time, at first looking out at the grass and trees and sky, and then, turning more and more into my mind and its noticing things, gradually looking at nothing of what was before my eyes. A great cutting slash arced across the last turn of the mental pathway I had wandered down and up, and was approaching me from the left. I cocked my head to that left. Slash, slash in the woods. My legs chilled. I will wait until I hear it once more, then I will get up and go inside.

Silence.

3

In times of trouble and despondency I turn to sportswear. I have just added to my wardrobe three pairs of pastel-colored shorts and four light-gray T shirts and a yellow cotton pullover so elegant and off-hand it must have been designed in France. I put on my new clothes, lace up my new white shoes, and see people. They say, "You look nice. Are those shorts new?"

"Yes, they are," I answer.

Then I go back home and sit on the porch under the sky in my new shorts.

4

I look at you sometimes when you're not aware of it. I look at you in those moments the way a stranger might so I can see you better than I usually do. And in fact you do always look fresh and new and similar to the person I think of as you. I love the way you look. And I feel happy just to be here looking at you, the way the dog sits at the feet of us, his great gods. I sit at the feet of the thing that is you. I look at your feet.

5

I take off my clothes and am in the air, me flowing through it and it flowing around me. I look to the right. The first cottages of the little village, the first houses of the town, the first buildings of the city: bones, flesh, and clothing. Air around it all. Air I cannot breathe, because I am also a structure I am moving past, a tomb, a monument, a big nothing.

6

He is a man of many vectors that assemble and reassemble, the way music comes first from the air, then from a piece of wood grown in air. Then the air is in a museum in a country you are not permitted to enter at this time because your vectors are not in order. You must go home and reassemble your rods and cones: night is falling, the soft gray mist of his breath.

7

I dreamed I had become a tall hamburger piloting a plane going down in a remote jungle waving up at me with inexpensive green cardboard natives ecstatic at the arrival, at last, of their messiah. A radiant hamburger bun top opened above me as I floated softly into their gyrating angular green midst.

8

I come to a mental clearing where I can speak only from the heart. Free of the baggage of who I happen to be, and of all the porters who must carry the baggage, and the exorbitant taxi ride into a fuller version of the same small personality, I take, for what seems to be the first time in a long time, a breath that goes deeper than the bottom of the lungs, and in the pause that comes at the end of that breath there appears a little mirror, light fog on it clearing quickly.

9

The palm of my hand is in Sunday, groggy, sabbatical. The rest of me is in Wednesday, up there and to the left, in the sky. I see you need a light, though you have nothing to smoke. You left your smoking utensils in Thursday. Let me recall my hand and fetch them for you. There, now you are creating puffs. But they do not dissipate. They form shadow copies of my hand that is moving toward your face.

10

It dawns on me that I'm repeating myself. Another day and there I am, calm outside in the air with my hand returning along its vectors. In this mental clearing the photons are jumping all around the savages. Suddenly the witch doctor brings his face to mine and shouts, "Mgwabi! Mgwabi!" pointing to my photons. I reach up and take the light from his face and fold it with the fingers on my hands and it dawns on me that I'm repeating myself.

11

At the end of the light I raise my voice from down there to up here and you are not here. I could shout until the words change colors and it would make no difference. Your vectors are heading out away from the voice of my hand and toward what it is pointing to, that bright cloud over there, the one with the burning edges, handsome and lighter than air at last.

12

A cold streak runs through the sky now the color of wet cement that forms the body of the man whose brain is at a height of more miles than can be found on earth. This emotional absolute zero is like a spine conducting thick fog and thin rain through him, and when the sun's vectors approach his surface they turn and move parallel to it. Who is this big cement man? And how do I know whether or not he is the same one who came this morning and threw on the power that sent the electricity branching through my heart?

13

It's dark today. I sit inside, my right hand touching my head. I look at the floor, the fabrics, the smoke from my mouth. It's as if there isn't any light, as if part of things being here is what light they have inseparable from themselves, not visible. The table doesn't stand for anything, although it remembers the tree. The table isn't immortal, though it hums a tune of going on forever. The table is in Friday, with me, both of us here in this dark miserable day, and I have the feeling I'm smiling, though I'm not.

Prose Poem

The morning coffee. I'm not sure why I drink it. Maybe it's the ritual of the cup, the spoon, the hot water, the milk, and the little heap of brown grit, the way they come together to form a nail I can hang the day on. It's something to do between being asleep and being awake. Surely there's something better to do, though, than to drink a cup of instant coffee. Such as meditate? About what? About having a cup of coffee. A cup of coffee whose first drink is too hot and whose last drink is too cool, but whose many in-between drinks are, like Baby Bear's porridge, just right. Papa Bear looks disgruntled. He removes his spectacles and swivels his eyes onto the cup that sits before Baby Bear, and then, after a discrete cough, reaches over and picks it up. Baby Bear doesn't understand this disruption of the morning routine. Papa Bear brings the cup close to his face and peers at it intently. The cup shatters in his paw, explodes actually, sending fragments and brown liquid all over the room. In a way it's good that Mama Bear isn't there. Better that she rest in her grave beyond the garden, unaware of what has happened to the world.

Talking to Vladimir Mayakovsky

All right, I admit it:
    It was just a dream I had last night.
        I was trudging along a muddy path
in a column of downcast men
    on the blackened outskirts of New York,
        the twilight dingy and ruined,
the future without hope
    as we marched along
        in our soiled, proletarian rags.
To my left was Mayakovsky, head shaved,
    and next to him his friend
        with gray beard and dark cap.
"You've got to admit," Mayakovsky
    was saying, "that this is a pretty good
        way to write a poem."
"Yes, " I said, "the momentum
    is sustained by our walking forward,
        the desolate landscape seeps into every word,
and you're free to say anything you want."
    "That's because we're inside the poem,"
        he said, "not outside." Puddles
of oily water gleamed dully beneath the low clouds.
    "That's why my poems were so big:
        there's more room *inside*."
The hard line of his jaw flexed and
    the men dispersed. I followed
        his friend behind a wall
to hear the poem go on
    in the lecture the friend was giving on history,
        but no, the real poem had finished.
I went back to the spot
    where the poem had finished.
        Vladimir had left the poem.

Flower's Escape

What have we here, a little daisy alongside the footpath, hmm. But as I bend to pick it, I pause, I freeze, I am a statue, and the daisy expands to the height of a man and begins to move off down the footpath, barely skimming the ground, its petals flared back in the breeze. But I don't mind. Being immobile like this will give me time to contemplate the eternity that lies before me, and whose silent voice insists on reminding me, from time to time, "Ron, you are not." Sometimes this happens when I've gone to bed and am lying there suddenly aware of how dark it is in the room; sometimes it happens when I'm driving along a country road, a ghost in my pickup truck! And I think how funny it is that I, who am not, am also a man driving a red truck, and the flexibility of my body is enjoying itself as I wind up and take the curves in a gentle centrifugal arc and my body weighs a little more on that side for a moment, and Nat "King" Cole is telling me I'm unforgettable, which I appreciate, although I know full well that I will be forgotten, unless I stay like this, bent over a flower that has fled my touch.

Fairy Tale

The little elf is dressed in a floppy cap
and he has a big rosy nose and flaring white eyebrows
with short legs and a jaunty step, though sometimes
he glides across an invisible pond with a bonfire glow on his cheeks:
it is northern Europe in the nineteenth century and people
are strolling around Copenhagen in the late afternoon,
mostly townspeople on their way somewhere,
perhaps to an early collation of smoked fish, rye bread, and cheese,
washed down with a dark beer: ha ha, I have eaten this excellent meal
and now I will smoke a little bit and sit back and stare down
at the golden gleam of my watch fob against the coarse dark wool of my vest,
and I will smile with a hideous contentment, because I am an evil man,
and tonight I will do something evil in this city!

Morning

Who is here with me?
My mother and an Indian man.
(I am writing this in the past.)
The Indian man is not a man,
but a wooden statue just outside
the limits of wood. My mother
is made of mother. She touches
the wood with her eyes and the eyes
of the statue turn to hers, that is,
become hers. (I am not dreaming.
I haven't even been born yet.)
There is a cloud in the sky.
My father is inside the cloud,
asleep. When he wakes up, he
will want coffee and a smoke.
My mother will set fire
to the Indian and from deep inside
her body I will tell her
to start the coffee, for even now
I hear my father's breathing change.

Bernadette Mayer

Bernadette Mayer was born in 1945 in Brooklyn. She studied at the New School for Social Research, graduating in 1967. That same year she co-founded, with the conceptual artist Vito Acconi, the magazine *0 to 9*, which published work by experimental artists in a variety of genres and media. In 1971 Mayer began teaching a series of extremely influential workshops at the St Mark's Poetry Project; these increasingly challenged what had become New York School orthodoxy – that is, the notion a poem should be witty, ludic, casual, immediate, irreverent, and anti-academic. Mayer's extensive reading lists featured texts by Wittgenstein, Barthes, Lacan, and Derrida, and she encouraged her students, who included a number of future Language writers (Charles Bernstein, Bruce Andrews, Nick Piombino, and Lisa Jarnot) to investigate the act of composition from a range of philosophical and theoretical perspectives. Her widely circulated compilation of 'Writing Experiments' include suggestions such as 'Attempt to eliminate all connotation from a piece of writing and vice versa'; these pushed numerous younger poets into unfamiliar territory, and have been borrowed by creative writing instructors around the world. Mayer was a very active director of St Mark's in the 1980s, and her United Artists Press published volumes by, among others, James Schuyler, Ron Padgett, Ted Berrigan, Bill Berkson, and Robert Creeley.

Mayer's own early work reveals a movement towards a spare, objective style, on which Gertude Stein is perhaps the dominant influence. Like Stein, Mayer often repeats words from a limited vocabulary, and her poems and prose texts conjugate a landscape or theme from a series of interlocking angles, or as part of an ongoing sequence. Mayer's books are often the result of a particular concept or experiment, in which writing may be only one element. In 1972, for instance, she had a show at a downtown gallery which consisted of an eight-hour tape of her reading a text based on her journal from the month of July 1971, and a vast display of photos taken that same month at the rate of thirty-six a day. Her 120-page *Midwinter Day* (1982) was written entirely on 22 December 1978, using notes, tapes, photographs and memory. Such projects serve to reformulate the relationship between life and art, and are a way of 'obfuscating', to use her own term, accepted literary and aesthetic conventions. 'The best obfuscation,' she writes, 'bewilders old meanings while reflecting or imitating or creating a structure of beauty that we know.' They are also designed to make poetry a part of ordinary existence, and to make ordinary existence the inescapable subject matter of poetry. Mayer's free flowing, diary-like sequences are beautifully quirky and alert transcriptions of what Elizabeth Bishop once called the 'surrealism of everyday life'.

Corn

Corn is a small hard seed.

Corn from Delft
Is good for elves.

White corn, yellow, Indian

Is this kernel a kernel of corn?

The corn they sought
Was sown by night.

The Corn Islands are two small islands,
Little Corn Island and Great Corn Island,
on an interoceanic canal route.

Any of several
insects that bore in maize is a corn borer.

America

As for me, when I saw you
You were in a tale
Thinking perhaps love is coming too
In America
Or perhaps as what is belated in a tale
May come true,
The scene is simply describing its use.

You had no hope
But the length of days, as in the sky
About which I already knew.

This gentle information
Comes as a prescription.

To notice a friend
Who is lettering a cloud
Which otherwise falls indifferently
Is no mark of distinction.
This is the difference
Between the past and dreams,
To dismiss an effigy
Which appears to be singing.

Index

a briar, a blunder, a
bungalow

-awning

briar
blunder
bungalow

Spelling is be-
coming more
Steward

tawdry

the blunder, a briar, a
bungalow
thigh

Tradition

tuck

Laura Cashdollars

cut mats are even
come to rest when
cut mats securing
the park bits to
poor Laura secure
as yet with still
less to neck than
the drink as four
corners the stick
to mix the fourth with.

Sea

It's he, it's sea. The sea is continuous; a continuous body. There was an Old Man of the Hague who is famous. What color is it? As you are when he's ashore. Wind is a natural motion of air. The numberless hues include gray, buff, slate, brown, and russet. Some winds blow all year in the same I direction. She came from the south.

With swords I am building an empire. Two drams borax, one dram alum, one dram camphor, one ounce sugar candy. The sea a continuous body of salt water covering three-fourths of the earth's surface. There was an Old Man of the Hague, whose ideas were excessively vague. Then when is a sailor like a beach? Hear when he's ashore, when he's aloft, when he's aboard, his diet, duties, and exercise. In atmosphere wind has speed, direction, and motion. The colors of salmon, faun, Esterhazy, lilac, green and maize, before the eyes. Winds of the same seasons and at the same hours of the day are periodic and never blinding. She came from the south, she arrived at her destination. It was winter.

One word follows the other with words. Repeat a ten minute stirring three times daily for two weeks. Sea and ocean are sometimes synonymous. A man from the Hague has built a balloon to examine the moon. There was an Old Man of the Hague. When is a sailor not a sailor? When else? If you want to know, when he was in the shrouds, since I've been at sea, they were riding the main, living on whale. The warmer air rose, the cold rushing in currents to fill the space. Full winds vary their directions change. She walked toward the house of the doctor who was singing.

With words you say and with pencils a drawing. Later a bell, a spill and a spell. Stir until clear and transparent. Hurricane winds blow sixty-four knots or more at sea. There was an Old Man from the Hague who built a balloon out of vague ideas. When is a sailor a corpse? Why are they always bad horsemen? The sailor muttered his health was better. The ship is adrift. The warmer air ascends. The Sargasso Sea is red and tints and shades of the same. Others are blue, green and Esterhazy all shades that vary. The doctor sang through the seasons. She broke the ice and threw it into the water, laying down a layer of blue earth.

A bell can't spell. We spell bell bell. It's he, it's sea. Strain, blot and bottle up for use. If too strong add water. The shore divides the land from the sea.

There was an Old Man from the Hague
Whose ideas were excessively vague;
He built a balloon
To examine the moon,
There was an Old Man from the Hague.

When is a boat like a heap of snow? What makes a road broad? If you want to know my health is good though I diet, sail and exercise. The ship now rests in the bosom of a cove. The winds are regular, periodic, and variable. We study colors. Some have slight motion some violent velocity. The rest of the story goes:

She put down a second layer of blue earth and a third. But the water still ran inland. So she put strips of basketry along the shore's length. The water ran through and out and came no further inland than where she had placed the basketry along the beaches. The blue earth could be seen. The ocean had retired.

It is not true that: where a warehouse is further a redder one may be laughed at. It is true that returning. Laughed at, one may be redder; further is a warehouse where . . .

Steps

steps, shops   noses, ears, eyes   steps
mouths, bills, beaks   shops
telephone   whiskers, horns, tufts   ships at sea
and telegraph   hair, fur, feathers   post cards
wires

hair, fur, feathers   a   protecting
1. short   b   insulating
2. medium
3. long   black hair, blue black wigs, hairpieces
brown hair, gray, light   (a) hoofs
brown, platinum hair,   (b) hoofs
1. blondes   reddish brown, yellow hair   tons of steel
2. brunettes
3. redheads

the palms of the hands   cleaning women
persons   soles of the feet   elevators
persons working

white space
microscopes   noses, ears, eyes
binoculars   windows
telescopes
crossed periscopes   black eyes, blue eyes are like cameras
eyes   brown eyes, gray eyes   i. blind
compound eyes   green eyes, red eyes   ii. color blind
floodlights   iii. myopic

lids, brows, lashes   observatory

antennas
nails, claws, wings   limbs
antlers, antennae, arms   visitors
color vision   legs, feet, hoofs, paws
5. sex   fangs, teeth
television tower
shedding
molting
shells, torsos, trunks   1. height
2. weight
3. color of eyes
4. color of hair

miles of pipeline

Poem

I am beginning to alter
The location of this harbor
Which now meets with a channel
Joining one place with another.
Then it continues
As if in a town
The artfulness of a hand
Full of some things
And not others.
The eye rests
And we see
What is before
Everything else the same.
Though this implies a beginning
To which we ascribe no point
Nevertheless it has an end,
For no bishop of any importance
Constructs his tomb in a bad time.

The end which comes
Is not as important as the motion
Held in the air
Pausing in its course.
To switch then
Reverses the train
Of a running line,
And as before
May wheel and address
To a new location
To be seen beneath.
This flying conversion
Sets the scene
To a bell.

I have told more
Than can be seen.
The bell makes its trick
More than an opera.
If you have seen the world from a ship
Then you have not seen

What the ship lets fall into the sea
To blacken its top and make it grow.
To get out of this seaport
You must be a cutter of networks.

The Incorporation of Sophia's Cereal

Two mad men and to mad men what poetry is
Fine lines written dumbfounded and high
& equally always the syncretistic goings-on
because everyone is furnishing everything
With the body they already have to live in
Beyond even believing in living, there was
This morning's bowl of puffed wheat, the bananas
Were the teachers, the cereals were the kids
And I Sophia said was the giant and
My spoon was my spoon

Max Carries the One

Dont look at me, look at your own self
In the given weather it's raining harder
The world is round & falling down, so rocks
Look out! it's nice to be exact as she & he
Fall like rain to a little bit lower than
Young & watching something without participating
Where you begin or above like snow flying up
The curve uncriticized by us, the child
The dumb drips exist when the sun
Beyond the stupid rectangles is the ancient flower
Shines on them? comes out; so what? criss-cross?

Counting nineteen humans plus eight trees equals
Twenty-seven living beings and that's all
And one is watching this something, you carry the one

Failures in Infinitives

why am i doing this? Failure
to keep my work in order so as
to be able to find things
to paint the house
to earn enough money to live on
to reorganize the house so as
to be able to paint the house &
to be able to find things and
earn enough money so as
to be able to put books together
to publish works and books
to have time
to answer mail & phone calls
to wash the windows
to make the kitchen better to work in
to have the money to buy a simple radio
to listen to while working in the kitchen
to know enough to do grownups work in the world
to transcend my attitude
to an enforced poverty
to be able to expect my checks
to arrive on time in the mail
to not always expect that they will not
to forget my mother's attitudes on humility or
to continue
to assume them without suffering
to forget how my mother taunted my father
about money, my sister about i cant say it
failure to forget mother and father enough
to be older, to forget them
to forget my obsessive uncle
to remember them some other way
to remember their bigotry accurately
to cease to dream about lions which always is
to dream about them, I put my hand in the lion's mouth
to assuage its anger, this is not a failure
to notice that's how they were; failure
to repot the plants
to be neat
to create & maintain clear surfaces

to let a couch or a chair be a place for sitting down
and not a table
to let a table be a place for eating & not a desk
to listen to more popular music
to learn the lyrics
to not need money so as
to be able to write all the time
to not have to pay rent, con ed or telephone bills
to forget parents' and uncle's early deaths so as
to be free of expecting care; failure
to love objects
to find them valuable in any way; failure
to preserve objects
to buy them and
to now let them fall by the wayside; failure
to think of poems as objects
to think of the body as an object; failure
to believe; failure
to know nothing; failure
to know everything; failure
to remember how to spell failure; failure
to believe the dictionary & that there is anything
to teach; failure
to teach properly; failure
to believe in teaching
to just think that everybody knows everything
which is not my failure; I know everyone does; failure
to see not everyone believes this knowing and
to think we cannot last till the success of knowing
to wash all the dishes only takes ten minutes
to write a thousand poems in an hour
to do an epic, open the unwashed window
to let in you know who and
to spirit thoughts and poems away from concerns
to just let us know, we will
to paint your ceilings & walls for free

Turning Prose into Poetry

a bird, probably a grackle, got caught in
the woodstove; we're afraid to open the door
prose above, poem below:
in june
the woodstove
sings like a bird

Maple Syrup Sonnet

for Grace

for over ten years now
if you can imagine that
confluence of the east and west
I have been wearing pearl river boxer shorts
they are like persian blue irises
no, hyacinths no midnight blue rooms

for eight years, willy-nilly
I've been trying to get more
    they are 100% cotton

if I were getting them for you
I would not only have them but see
a plethora of wonderful things that day

today we are making maple syrup again
I pray for them
                    our father who art in heaven
                    please get me some maple syrup 100% cotton
                    boxer shorts because of the war amen

Maple Syrup Sonnet

syrup's up again
day dawns gloomy but birds
have found the feeder at last, march 22, 2003
of course there's a war
bush says, the war is going well
phil's tending the evaporator fire
now he's cleaning & raking
things we didn't do:
rake, reiki, make war on iraq
sophie & zac arrive, our premier
evaporator tenders & mood elevators
let's go. first I eat sweet
maple syrup tapioca, birds gather
in the nearby sycamore tree, then flee
to eat maple syrup over LSD

Palm Sunday Maple Syrup Poem

a poem is like a palm
in that it is sap evaporating
like a horse in a corral
running frenetically to the road when
a car approaches like a bird
who comes to the feeder despite
the hot sweet smoke, should we end today
if you end one thing, you might end
another like the winter or the life
of a traitor humming like a cloud
in the clear blue sky's use
of a plateau to warmer, itchy weather
when we can swim in the creek
beyond the field behind the day's evaporator, amen

Booze Turns Men into Women

A sip of Coors makes children be
Nuclear power plant contractors
Wild Turkey turns men into deer
Molson's Canadian Beer makes
All the people fear laundromats
Stolichnaya turns women into Rolling Rocks
Men turn women into oatmeal stout
Jack Daniels turns men into Queen Anne's lace
Triple Sec turns men into margaritas
Der Budweiser juven often undoes mein leben
Grand Marnier turns women into
ancient mariners
Crème de Cassis creates
Child toxic waste entrepreneurs
Watney's weakens warriors
A taste of jeniver turned Beatrice into a t-square
Martell's makes men Mooseheads
Heinekens dimwit God couscous miracle elf
Gins turn men into safety pins
Chivas Regal makes men sewing needles
Blackeyed Susans turn men into Jack Daniels
Women wake from highballs as walnuts
Cocktails alienate communalists and
A glass of Schaeffer'll
Make your kid a general

SELECT BIBLIOGRAPHY

Edwin Denby

Poetry

In Public, In Private (Prairie City, IL: The Press of James A. Decker, 1948)
Mediterranean Cities (New York: Wittenborn, 1956)
C Magazine, Vol. 1, No. 4, Special Denby Issue (New York: September 1963)
Snoring in New York (New York: Angel Hair / Adventures in Poetry, 1974)
Collected Poems (New York: Full Court Press, 1975)
The Complete Poems (New York: Random House, 1986)

Criticism

Ballet (New York: J.J. Augustin, 1945)
Looking at the Dance (New York: Pellegrini and Cudahy, 1949; New York: Popular Library, 1978)
Dancers, Buildings and People in the Streets (New York: Horizon, 1965; New York: Popular Library, 1979)
Dance Writings (New York: Knopf, 1986)

Barbara Guest

Poetry

The Location of Things (New York: Tibor de Nagy, 1960)
Poems: The Location of Things, Archaics, The Open Skies (Garden City, NY: Doubleday, 1962)
The Blue Stairs (New York: Corinth Books, 1968)
Moscow Mansions (New York: Viking, 1973)
The Countess from Minneapolis (Providence, RI: Burning Deck, 1976)
The Türler Losses (Montreal: Mansfield Book Mart, 1979)
Biography (Providence, RI: Burning Deck, 1980)

Quilts (New York: Vehicle Editions, 1981)
Fair Realism (Los Angeles: Sun & Moon Press, 1989)
Defensive Rapture (Los Angeles: Sun & Moon Press, 1992)
Selected Poems (Los Angeles: Sun & Moon Press, 1995; Manchester: Carcanet, 1995)
If So, Tell Me (London: Reality Street Editions, 1999)
Rocks on a Platter: Notes on Literature (Middletown, CT: Wesleyan University Press, 1999)
Miniatures and Other Poems (Middletown, CT: Wesleyan University Press, 2002)
The Red Gaze (Middletown, CT: Wesleyan University Press, 2005)

Fiction

Seeking Air (Los Angeles: Black Sparrow, 1978)

Criticism

Herself Defined: The Poet H.D. and Her World (New York: Quill, 1985)
Durer in the Window: Reflexions on Art (New York: Roof Books, 2003)
Forces of Imagination: Writing on Writing (Berkeley, CA: Kelsey Street Press, 2003)

Kenward Elmslie

Poetry

Motor Disturbance (New York: Columbia University Press, 1971)
Circus Nerves (Los Angeles: Black Sparrow Press, 1971)
The Orchid Stories (New York: Doubleday, 1973)
Tropicalism (Calais, VT: Z Press, 1975)
Communications Equipment (Providence, RI: Burning Deck, 1979)
Moving Right Along (Calais, VT: Z Press, 1980)
Bare Bones (Flint, MI: Bamberger Books, 1995)
Routine Disruptions: Selected Poems and Lyrics 1960–1998 (Minneapolis: Coffee House Press, 1998)
Blast From the Past (Austin: Skanky Possum, 2000)

Harry Mathews

Poetry

The Ring: Poems 1956–1969 (Leeds: Juillard, 1970)
The Planisphere (Providence, RI: Burning Deck, 1977)
Trial Impressions (Providence, RI: Burning Deck, 1977)
Armenian Papers: Poems 1954–1984 (Princeton: Princeton University Press, 1987)
Out of Bounds (Providence, RI: Burning Deck, 1989)
A Mid-Season Sky: Poems 1954–1991 (Manchester: Carcanet Press, 1992)

Fiction

The Conversions (New York: Random House, 1962; Normal, IL: Dalkey Archive Press, 1997)
Tlooth (New York: Doubleday, 1966; Normal, IL: Dalkey Archive Press, 1998)
Country Cooking and Other Stories (Providence, RI: Burning Deck, 1980)
The Sinking of the Odradek Stadium (New York: Harper & Row, 1975; Normal, IL: Dalkey Archive Press, 1999)
Cigarettes (New York: Weidenfeld and Nicholson, 1987; Normal, IL: Dalkey Archive Press, 1998)
The Journalist (Boston: Godine, 1994; Normal, IL: Dalkey Archive Press, 1997)
The Human Country: New and Collected Stories (Normal, IL: Dalkey Archive Press, 2002)
My Life in CIA (Normal, IL: Dalkey Archive Press, 2005)

Criticism

The Case of the Persevering Maltese: Collected Essays (Normal, IL: Dalkey Archive Press, 2002)

Ted Berrigan

Poetry

The Sonnets (New York: C Press, 1964; New York: Grove Press, 1967; New York: Penguin, 2000)
Living with Chris (New York: Boke Press, 1965)

Bean Spasms (with Ron Padgett) (New York: Kulchur Press, 1968)
Many Happy Returns (New York: Corinth Books,1967)
In the Early Morning Rain (London: Cape Goliard Press, 1970)
Memorial Day (with Anne Waldman) (London: Aloes Press, 1974)
A Feeling for Leaving (New York: Frontward Books, 1975)
Red Wagon (Chicago: Yellow Press, 1976)
Clear the Range (New York: Adventures in Poetry / Coach House South, 1977)
Nothing for You (Lenox, MA: Angel Hair Books, 1977)
So Going Around Cities: New and Selected Poems 1958–1979 (Berkeley, CA: Blue Wind Press, 1980)
A Certain Slant of Sunlight (Oakland, CA: O Books, 1988)
Selected Poems (New York: Penguin, 1994)
The Collected Poems of Ted Berrigan (Berkeley, CA: University of California Press, 2005)

Joseph Ceravolo

Poetry

Fits of Dawn (New York: C Press, 1965)
Wild Flowers Out of Gas (New York: Tibor de Nagy Editions, 1967)
Spring In This World of Poor Mutts (New York: Columbia University Press, 1968)
INRI (Putnam Valley, NY: Swollen Magpie Press, 1979)
Transmigration Solo (West Branch, IA: The Toothpaste Press, 1979)
The Green Lake Is Awake (Minneapolis: Coffee House Press, 1994)

Bill Berkson

Poetry

Saturday Night: Poems 1960–61 (New York: Tibor de Nagy, 1961)
Shining Leaves (New York: Angel Hair Books, 1969)
Recent Visitors (New York: Angel Hair Books, 1973)
Enigma Variations (Bolinas, CA: Big Sky, 1975)
Blue Is the Hero (Kensington, CA: L Publications, 1975)
Lush Life (Calais, VT: 2 Press, 1983)
Serenade (Cambridge, MA: Zoland, 2000)
Fugue State (Cambridge, MA: Zoland, 2002)
Hymns of St. Bridget and Other Writings (with Frank O'Hara) (The Owl Press, 2003)

Criticism

The Sweet Singer of Modernism and Other Art Writings (Jamestown, RI: Qua Books, 2004)

Clark Coolidge

Poetry

Flag Flutter and U.S. Electric (New York: Lines Books, 1966)
Clark Coolidge (New York: Lines Books, 1967)
Ing (New York: Angel Hair Books, 1968)
Space (New York: Harper & Row, 1970)
The So: Poems 1966 (New York: Adventures in Poetry, 1971)
The Maintains (San Francisco: This Press, 1974)
Polaroid (New York: Adventures in Poetry / Bolinas, CA: Big Sky, 1975)
Own Face (Lenox, MA: Angel Hair Books, 1978)
Quartz Hearts (San Francisco: This Press, 1978)
Smithsonian Depositions / Subject to a Film (New York: Vehicle Editions, 1980)
Mine: The One That Enters The Stories (Berkeley, CA: The Figures, 1982)
The Crystal Text (Great Barrington, MA: The Figures, 1986)
Solution Passage: Poems 1978–1981 (Los Angeles: Sun & Moon Press, 1986)
Sound as Thought: Poems 1982–1984 (Los Angeles: Sun & Moon Press, 1990)
Odes of Roba (Great Barrington, MA: The Figures, 1991)
The Book of During (Great Barrington, MA: The Figures, 1991)
The ROVA Improvisations (Los Angeles: Sun & Moon Press, 1994)
The Book of Stirs (Los Angeles: Seeing Eye Books, 1998)
Now It's Jazz (Albuquerque, NM: Living Batch, 1999)
Alien Tatters (Berkeley, CA: Atelos, 2000)
On the Nameways, vols 1 and 2 ((Great Barrington, MA: The Figures, 2000, 2001)
Far Out West (New York: Adventures in Poetry, 2002)
On the Slates (Oakland, CA: Tougher Disguises, 2002)

Charles North

Poetry

Lineups (New York: Self-published, 1972)
Elizabethan & Nova Scotian Music (New York: Adventures in Poetry, 1974)

Six Buildings (Putnam Valley, NY: The Swollen Magpie Press, 1977)
Leap Year: Poems 1968–1978 (New York: The Kulchur Foundation, 1978)
Gemini (with Tony Towle) (Putnam Valley, NY: Swollen Magpie, 1981)
The Year of the Olive Oil (Brooklyn: Hanging Loose Press, 1989)
New and Selected Poems (Los Angeles: Sun & Moon Press, 1999)
The Nearness of the Way You Look Tonight (New York: Adventures in Poetry, 2000)
Tulips (New Haven, CT: Phylum Press, 2004)

Criticism

No Other Way: Selected Prose (Brooklyn: Hanging Loose Press, 1998)

Ron Padgett

Poetry

Great Balls of Fire (Chicago: Holt, Rinehart & Winston, 1969; Minneapolis: Coffee House Press, 1990)
Toujours l'amour (New York : SUN, 1976)
Tulsa Kid (Calais, VT : Z Press, 1979)
Triangles in the Afternoon (New York: SUN, 1979)
The Big Something (Great Barrington, MA: The Figures, 1990)
New and Selected Poems (Boston: David R. Godine, 1995)
Poems I Guess I Wrote (New York: Cuz Editions, 2001)
You Never Know (Minneapolis: Coffee House Press, 2002)

Criticism and Memoirs

Blood Work: Selected Prose (Flint, MI: Bamberger Books, 1993)
Ted: A Personal Memoir of Ted Berrigan (Great Barrington, MA: The Figures, 1993)
Albanian Diary (Great Barrington, MA: The Figures, 1999)
The Straight Line: Writings on Poetry and Poets (Ann Arbor: University of Michigan Press, 2000)
Oklahoma Tough (Tulsa: University of Oklahoma, 2003)
Joe: A Memoir of Joe Brainard (Minneapolis: Coffee House Press, 2004)

Bernadette Mayer

Poetry

Story (New York: 0 to 9 Press, 1968)
Moving (New York: Angel Hair Books, 1971)
Memory (Plainfield, VT: North Atlantic Books, 1976)
Ceremony Latin (1964) (New York: Angel Hair Books, 1975)
Studying Hunger (New York: Adventures in Poetry / Bolinas, CA: Big Sky, 1976)
Poetry (New York: Kulchur Foundation, 1976)
Eruditio Ex Memoria (Lenox, MA: Angel Hair, 1977)
The Golden Book of Words (Lenox, MA: Angel Hair, 1978)
Midwinter Day (Berkeley, CA: Turtle Island Foundation, 1982)
Utopia (New York: United Artists Books, 1984)
Sonnets (New York: Tender Buttons, 1989)
The Formal Field of Kissing (New York: Catchword Papers, 1990)
A Bernadette Mayer Reader (New York: New Directions, 1992)
The Desires of Mothers to Please Others in Letters (West Stockbridge, MA: Hard Press, 1994)
Proper Name and other stories (New York: New Directions, 1996)
Another Smashed Pinecone (New York: United Artists Books, 1998)
Two Haloed Mourners: Poems (New York: Granary Books, 1998)
Indigo Bunting (La Laguna, Canary Islands: Zasterle Press, 2004)
Scarlet Tanager (New York: New Directions, 2005)

INDEX OF FIRST LINES

INDEX OF TITLES

ACKNOWLEDGEMENTS

The editors would especially like to acknowledge the assistance of Larry Fagin, who generously made his library available to us.

We are grateful to the authors and publishers of the poems in this anthology for permission to reprint previously published material.

EDWIN DENBY: poems by Edwin Denby from *The Complete Poems* (New York: Random House, 1986) Copyright © 1975 by Edwin Denby. Used by permission of the Estate of Edwin Denby, Yvonne Jacquette Burckhardt, executor.

BARBARA GUEST: 'Parachutes, My Love, Could Carry Us Higher', 'The Farewell Stairway', 'Dissonance Royal Traveller' from *Selected Poems* © Barbara Guest 1962, 1989, 1992, 1996, reprinted by permission of Carcanet Press; 'Twilight Polka Dots', Outside of This, That Is' © Barbara Guest 2006; 'Blurred Edge', in *Miniatures and Other Poems* © 2002 by Barbara Guest and reprinted by permission of Wesleyan University Press; 'Nostalgia of the Infinite and 'The Hungry Knight' in *The Red Gaze* © 2005 by Barbara Guest and reprinted with permission of Wesleyan University Press.

KENWARD ELMSLIE: Poems © Kenward Elmslie 2006.

HARRY MATHEWS: 'The Relics', Invitation to a Sabbath', 'Comatas', 'The Ring' from *A Mid Season Sky* © Harry Mathews 1992, reprinted by permission of Carcanet Press; ''Spell', 'The Sense of Responsibility', 'The Ledge', 'Cassation on a Theme by Jacques Dupin', 'The Dream-Work', 'Lateral Disregard' © Harry Mathews 2006.

TED BERRIGAN: 'Sonnet I', 'Sonnet XVII', 'Sonnet XXIII', 'Sonnet XXX', 'Sonnet XXXVI', 'Sonnet XXXVII', 'Sonnet LV', 'Sonnet LIX', 'Sonnet LXXIV', Sonnet 'LXXVI' from *The Sonnets* by Ted Berrigan, copyright © 2000 by Alice Notley, Literary Executrix of the Estate of Ted Berrigan. Used by permission of Viking Penguin, a division of Penguin Group (USA) Inc. 'Words for Love', 'Personal Poem # 7', 'Personal Poem # 8', 'Living with Chris', 'American Express', 'I Remember', 'Whitman in Black', 'Last Poem', excerpted from *The Collected Poems of Ted Berrigan*, by Ted Berrigan, published by the University of California Press © 2005 by the Regents of the University of California.